Uncuffed Potential

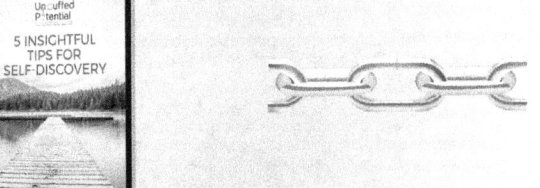

Uncuffed
Potential

5 INSIGHTFUL
TIPS FOR
SELF-DISCOVERY

Expand your knowledge even more with an additional resource from Curtis Ghee!

Uncuffing your potential involves looking within and going through the important and valuable process of self-discovery. To spark that inner growth so that you can reach your potential, Ghee has created an additional eBook for you with his top 5 insightful tips for self-discovery. The eBook also includes workbook components, inviting you to reflect and put in the effort for your growth. Take your personal development one step further!

Uncuffed Potential - Free your mind, change your life.
Copyright © Curtis Ghee

Published and printed by Ignite Publishing a division of JBO Global Inc.
5569-47th Street Red Deer, AB
Canada, T4N1S1 1-877-677-6115

Cover design by Dania Zafar
Book design by Dania Zafar and JB Owen
Edited by JB Owen and Mimi Safiyah
Designed in the United States of America, Printed in China
ISBN: 979-8-9872121-0-3

First edition

Ordering Information: Quantity sales. Special discounts are available on quantity purchases by corporations, associations, and others. For details, contact the publisher at the above address. Programs, products, or services provided by the author are found by contacting them directly. Resources named in the are found in the resources pages at the back of the book.

Author Details: Curtis Ghee

Uncuffed Potential

FREE YOUR MIND, CHANGE YOUR LIFE

CURTIS GHEE

TESTIMONIALS

This is hands-down the most inspirational book I have read in a very long time.

Curtis provides a wealth of examples, case studies, and anecdotes. With each one, he masterfully removes a brick from the wall you may have put up which made stepping up and into the life you want to live appear unrealistic or merely a dream.

Through his sincere, skillful, and inspirational storytelling, Curtis effortlessly reels you in and washes away any fears or uncertainty about taking the all-important leap into the future you want to build for yourself. You may have previously thought it was not possible, or was something that only the select few manage to achieve.

Reading 'Uncuffed Potential, Free Your Mind, Change Your Life—I felt like I was sitting with Curtis, listening to him share his life experience and top-tier coaching, and showing me that I have within me everything I need to live with great purpose and potential.

Absolutely a must-read for anyone who wants more out of life.

Tracy Stone, CL.Hyp, CPPD, ARTT, GHR (Reg.)

What an inspiring and motivating account of what can happen when someone discovers their purpose. A must-read for anyone experiencing difficulty finding meaning and purpose in their work. Masterfully done!

Pastor Norman C. Davenport

This book expresses the essence of Christian life and the importance of knowing and loving yourself. The quotes from the Bible and testimonial quotes fit together perfectly. Great work!

Deacon Larry Buck

Every few years a creative thinker emerges with a refreshing approach about discovering the formula for a purposeful and satisfying life; *Uncuffed Potential* sets itself apart from the typical self-help book. Readers will find themselves challenged and inspired to recognize and refocus their thinking about their own potential by providing real-life examples. Curtis Ghee humanizes and normalizes feeling lost, off track, and sometimes bound by other thinking. The uncuffing reference represents freedom. There is freedom offered in the pages of this book. He so eloquently encourages readers to take agency over their thinking, open themselves to receive the keys to uncuff their potential. Freedom resides there.

Dr. Shelita Jackson

This book was enlightening and thought provoking. My purpose for my life is clear and this book was helpful with executing my goals.

The author was thoughtful with the story's in this book. I looked forward to the quotes in each chapter. It was really insightful and I was excited to keep turning the pages.

Renee Cunningham

A true testimony of experience, strength and hope! Curtis Ghee takes you through this journey page by page that will truly light you up and transform your life: a book to not only read but share.

Dr. Jo Dee Baer

Curtis Ghee has written a powerful roadmap to finding your life purpose, forgiving past shortcomings, and acknowledging that you deserve all the riches that life has to offer. Curtis weaves uplifting stories and quotes that encourage us to reframe our current mindset and realize we can obtain anything we desire. This book is about second chances, and the gifts that unfold when we decide to live freely and unbound by our own fear and apprehension.

Cindy Tank-Murphy, Author, Speaker, Mental Health Advocate, & Energy Healer

Reading this book helped me realize the power of our potential. One thing in particular that stood out to me, was when Curtis found himself in a career that wasn't fulfilling him. Instead of giving up, or continuing his life the way it was, he took on the personal responsibility to take it a step further and create a ministry. As someone who is also in a helping profession, I've watched how so many people are just 'going with the motions' not realizing how much our clients really need us. I love the transition from transactional to transformational relationships that took place as I read about Curtis's life. Not only that, I love the actionable steps that he gives to help others live a fulfilling life. I definitely recommend this book to anyone who feels stuck, just like Curtis did, and from the wisdom within these pages, I hope you step forward in your unlimited potential.

Jessica T. Moore, MSW

Uncuffed Potential gave me such inspiration. Wonderful thought-provoking wisdom, inspiration, and motivation throughout. Appreciated Curtis's openness in incorporating personal stories in each chapter. This is a must-read by everyone.

Steph Elliot

CONTENTS

DEDICATION

I dedicate this book to my parents, the late Cornell Ghee Sr. and Shirley Ghee, for giving me life and provisions, as well as my siblings, Deborah, Lorraine, Constance, and my brother/hero, the late Cornell Jr., who all played a significant role in my upbringing. Also, I thank my lovely children Tamika, Briyonna, Curtis Jr., and Colin for enhancing my life.

Last but not least, I dedicate this book to my beautiful wife, Falesha, for always being in my corner, inspiring me and making my life that much better.

THANK YOU, LORD, FOR YOUR INSPIRATION!!!

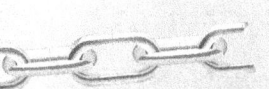 

FOREWORD
BY
DR. BRANVILLE G. BARD, JR.

"We all come to a place in our lives where we aspire to be that person that we believe we can someday be. The keys in this book will help you unlock your Potential and find your destiny."

~Dr. Branville G. Bard, Jr.

I had the life-enhancing opportunity of meeting Curtis Ghee nearly twenty years ago. At that time, he was serving as a police officer in one of the most challenging areas of an urban population center in Philadelphia, Pennsylvania, USA. There, as his commanding officer, I had the great fortune of being able to work closely with Curtis and see up close how his selflessness enhanced police-community relations and impacted the city in unparalleled ways.

Curtis's greatest strength as a police officer was also his greatest weakness as a person; you see, it always felt to me like Curtis held the Community by the same handle we typically hold family by; personal and interpersonal. We all know family can be some of the most uplifting and burdensome individuals in our lives. Curtis enjoyed a similar symbiotic relationship with the community. He rejoiced when the Community excelled, but he also hurt deeply when any part of them suffered or failed. Sadly, pain was far more prevalent than occasions to rejoice, but still, he persevered, giving more to his Community than he could ever recoup.

Much of Curtis' professional and adult life was devoted to encouraging others to pursue dreams he personally relished but would come to realize he was afraid to seek for himself. Nevertheless, the more Curtis persevered in his position, the more he grew as a leader. He was also a great role model to his peers, and as a senior officer, Curtis helped cultivate many younger officers. In the second half of his career, he joined the police department's counseling unit, where he counseled officers for stress, trauma, and other issues. Curtis's entire career was centered around empowering others.

When I began reading his book, I was captivated by the practical and relatable antidotes Curtis shared from beginning to end. *Uncuffed Potential* represents Curtis pouring his lived experience into the reader, providing them with the strength and tools they need to realize their dreams. He shows how one can triumph and escape from the internal prison they have built with their own hands. Through compelling and enlightening principles, Curtis empowers and uplifts everyone who reads this book, just as he continues to do in his Community.

As an educator and former Police Chief, I can attest to the fact that having a healthy *Perspective* of yourself, being *Passionate* about what you do, understanding *Potential* and *Purpose*, as well as having a *Plan* for your life are the essentials to your success. These fundamental concepts that Curtis masterfully captured in this book have helped me throughout my life and allowed me to experience great success. I know that if you apply them, everything in your life will be magnified.

Dr. Branville G. Bard, Jr.

Vice President of Public Safety for John Hopkins University| Medicine; Former Police Commissioner at Cambridge Police Department in Massachusetts

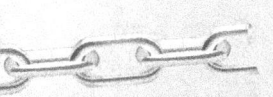

PREFACE

By the grace of God, I have never been arrested or spent a moment behind bars. Throughout my life, I have had the privilege to come and go as I desired. I believed that I lived a life without restrictions because I was physically free. But on the contrary, my mind was locked up in a maximum-security prison, often visited by my unfulfilled dreams, lost visions, failed ideas, and many wasted opportunities. Unfortunately, all of my high aspirations were vastly overshadowed by their cellmates: fear, doubt, regret, and feelings of inadequacy. At a point, I was lost, stuck, and drowning in a life of uncertainty. I could not see myself being the successful person I desired to be, and because of that, I remained locked up in that proverbial jail cell that I so desperately wanted to be freed from.

By the time I graduated high school in 1986 at age 17, my parents had divorced, and it was just my mom, and I left at home. I was a bright student, but to the surprise of many, I decided not to attend college. I had several opportunities to play football at a few of the state colleges that were offering athletic scholarships, but instead, I began working at a nursing home in a housekeeping position that started me off at minimum wage. Even though cleaning bathrooms and hauling trash was not what I had in mind fresh out of high school, it felt good to have my own job. I enjoyed the responsibility and was able to help my mom with the bills and buy myself a used car. It wasn't my dream job, but it was an honest way to earn a living until I figured out what I wanted for my life.

After working for about 18 months, I began to get a little nervous because of the looming uncertainty of what my future held that hovered over me. I was often reminded by my older coworkers, many of them old enough to be my grandparents, not to get stuck working at the nursing home. It was as though I was this young inmate doing a short time in prison, being mentored by senior inmates who were working through a life sentence of their own without the possibility of parole. The thought of spending the next 40 years of my life in a dead-end job was frightening to me. Unfortunately, at that point, I still had no idea what I wanted to do and thus stayed where I was.

A few years later, I ran into an old friend who was a Philadelphia police officer. He shared with me the particulars of being an officer and encouraged me to apply to take the next written exam. So, I did, and I found a job in law enforcement that I loved. Although it was full of excitement, I felt no closer to my purpose than when I was a kid in high school or when I was mopping floors and dumping trash at the nursing home. Was I any different from the guys and girls I was arresting who clearly lived a life without intent? What was my excuse? I had a good upbringing and a decent level of education. I felt like I should have been much further along in my life at that point, but I wasn't. Yes, I looked the part as though I had it all together, but I didn't. I wore that proverbial mask to hide behind my insecurities. My mind was no more liberated than any of the individuals that I was handcuffing and placing behind bars. Who was Curtis Ghee outside of the uniform, without the badge and gun? Despite the arrest powers given to me by the Commonwealth of Pennsylvania, I felt absolutely shackled and powerless in my personal life!

Then one day, it happened. It was a slightly warm Sunday afternoon when my heart was deeply touched by a tragedy that took place. There was a young man (I will refer to as Steve) who had just left church to order food from a fast-food takeout just 1/4 of a mile away from the church. While standing in the store waiting for his food, another young man came into the store with revenge in his heart. With an automatic weapon in hand, his intention was to shoot another young man to avenge being shot two years prior. Although he did shoot and wound his intended target, sadly he also shot Steve while he was waiting for his food. My partner and I were on patrol just minutes away from the scene when we received the emergency call. Upon our arrival, we found Steve gravely wounded. Amazingly, he ran from the store and collapsed on the front steps of the church he had attended. Despite the efforts of the responded medical staff, Steve was pronounced dead at the scene.

This was an incident where two young men inadvertently met for a *brief* moment that would change their lives and mine for a lifetime. This tragedy resulted in one young man ending up in a cemetery, and the other with a life sentence behind prison walls. As for me, the emotions behind this sad event and the subsequent murder trial left me wondering, What can I do differently? What can I do other than arrest people?

A few days after the commencement of the trial, I emailed my pastor and informed her that I felt compelled to start a prison ministry. She was ecstatic about the idea, and along with two other ministers in our congregation, we started the ministry in the spring of 2004 at one of the all-male facilities.

At that stage in my life, I was no longer just a cop. I discovered that although I had the power to handcuff and arrest people, *my true power was to influence and help them to unlock their potential!* As my career progressed, I became dedicated to working with the community and forged great relationships with residents and neighborhood leaders. My mantra was, 'Everyone has a story to tell,' meaning that we all have a backstory that played a role in the good and the bad in our lives. I strongly believe that if a person's mind is freed, their behavior can change for the better. My desire to make arrests became overshadowed by a yearning to make a difference.

The catalyst for writing this book came about when the director of Temple University's Pan African Studies program asked me to create a 45-minute seminar to encourage ex-offenders who were returning to society. Ironically, most of the 33 attendees were not ex-offenders, but they were drawn to the title, "The Five Keys to Your Destiny, "Free Your Mind, Change Your Life. "Coincidentally, I woke up the morning of the seminar and told my wife that I dreamed I had written a book based on the symposium. Hours later, after the session, I read an evaluation from a woman who attended that stated, "If Curtis has not written a book on this topic, then he should!" Confirmation!!! I realized that day that many people were in the same predicament I once found myself in. They, too, were seeking to discover who they were destined to become.

Today, I thank God that my mind is no longer bound as I discovered that my purpose was never outside of me, but instead, it was *within* me. Now I can view myself as a person who can accomplish anything I put my mind to.

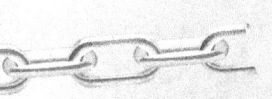

WHO SHOULD READ THIS BOOK

This book is for all the people who are unsatisfied with where they are at this juncture of their life, and do not know what steps to take to make a significant change. I know this feeling all too well, as I confess to you that for many years I also found myself feeling depleted and perplexed while stumbling through life. I was always starting over and over again and getting nowhere, never making it to where I wanted to get to. I had plenty of gas. I had the vehicle to take me there. Nevertheless, I found myself going past the same landmarks in the same environment year after year because I had no navigation system to direct me in the pathway of success. This left me feeling inadequate and frustrated as I'd watch others around me continuously reach their desired destinations.

Being sick and tired of watching others succeed while you are stuck in neutral does not make you a hater, but it does make you hate that part of yourself that is restricting you from becoming the person God designed for you to be. You have to reach a point where you stand up for yourself and tell the timid, lazy, undisciplined, doubtful you to *get moving*! My transformation came once I decided that I did not want to die with the gifts and talents that God gave me to impact the world. I was determined not to leave this planet without enjoying the life I desired to live and to leave a legacy for my family. I have no doubt that you, too, feel the same way I did, and you are seeking the same kind of personal joy and success in your life.

To educate and inspire myself I began to read books, watch videos and podcasts of successful people who accomplished the things that I wanted to achieve. I watched people who made it through adversities and overcame low self-esteem. I studied individuals who were able to share how they discovered their purpose and took action to obtain the life they desired. Most importantly, as a believer in the word of God, I began to live my life demonstrating that I truly believed the promises and principles in the Bible were true, and that they also applied to me. I began to realize that having faith, even as tiny as a mustard seed, could influence mountain-sized situations in my life. I trusted that with God, all things were possible, and once I could begin to see myself according to how He saw me, I could view myself from a better perspective.

If you are uncertain of your purpose, please do not be hard on yourself or ashamed. Remember, no manufacturer creates a product without revealing its purpose to its consumer. With that in mind, know that you are God's greatest creation, skillfully crafted and wired for success. Everything you need to succeed in life is already inside of you, batteries included! You may need some help learning how to use those skills to uncover your potential.

In this book, I will show you five fundamental principles that will help revolutionize your life. They will give you a pinpoint insight into the destiny that God placed explicitly in you. They represent *Perspective, Passion, Potential, Purpose,* and *Planning* and will show you how to view things with more clarity and confidence. They will inspire you to realize that having what you want is possible and that you can enjoy your life in the process. These principles will bring about self-discovery and give you a focus to help you achieve your destiny.

As you read each chapter, you will hear enlightening anecdotes about everyday people who faced difficulties head-on and rose to the occasion. My hope is as you read these personal stories, you will find your voice to tell your own story to help liberate someone else. You will learn that despite where you are in life, you are never too old to discover your purpose or utilize the potential you possess. You, too, are likely to want a better life, but are you willing to put in the work to create the life you want for yourself? Are you hungry enough to fight through difficult times without giving up? Remember, these principles will work *only* if you work them. They worked for me, they worked for others, and they can work for you. So, I challenge you to incorporate these five keys daily to *Uncuff Your Potential* so you, too, can manifest the life you desire. I know you wouldn't be here if you didn't desire more in your life, so let's roll up our sleeves and get started!

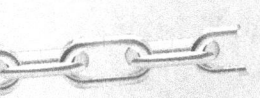

CHAPTER I

AWAKEN YOUR PERSPECTIVE

If you change the way you look at things,
the things you look at will change.

Dr. Wayne Dyer,

an American self-help Author and Motivational Speaker.

A person's philosophy can play a major role in how they behave. Whether you think highly of yourself or you struggle to believe that you have a bright future, more than likely, how you feel will dictate your conduct and actions. It can be quite a task trying to help someone see the world differently unless they are willing to change the story they believe.

For instance, a set of twin brothers had a drunkard for a father. One brother grew up to be an alcoholic, and when asked why he became a drunk, he responded, "Because my father was a drunk." The other twin grew up to become a successful businessman, and when asked why he became a successful businessman, he responded, "Because my father was a drunk." Here you have two men, both brought up under the same circumstances, but they see things from two totally different perspectives. According to their own beliefs, their behaviors manifested and produced a productive life for one and a non-productive outcome for the other. Bear in mind, you become what you think of yourself, so why not think highly of yourself?

YOUR PERSPECTIVE FRAMES YOUR WORLD

I am going to assume that if you are reading this book, then you are probably experiencing some uncertainty concerning your future. Whether you are a person from an upper-middle-class family or someone that grew up accustomed to struggling throughout life, your concept of *self* is what will determine your destination. You may feel inadequate based on what you have been taught or told. You might think that no one from your family or community has ever achieved anything close to what you imagine yourself achieving because you have never witnessed it in your lifetime. However, I want you to know that what you believe and say about yourself matters most! How you view your life and circumstances will determine whether or not your dreams and aspirations will become a reality or will only be a fantasy. That is why right here, I want you to decide that you will *only* speak words of positive affirmation that align with what you desire for your life and the goals you will set to get there. I want you to have a winning perspective that gives you the confidence that you can and will accomplish everything you desire. Your perspective is the key that unlocks the future that you've always dreamed of having. Therefore, I strongly encourage you to clear your mind of past and present issues, find a quiet place to collect your thoughts and allow yourself to imagine yourself being the person you desire to become. Picture yourself as the CEO of your own company, wearing that power suit and stilettos, standing with your arms folded. Fantasize about living in the home of your dreams and driving the car you've always wanted. Uncuff your imagination and give yourself permission to dream again. Quit worrying about what others think of you. Your perspective of you is the only one that matters.

What is perspective? A perspective is simply someone's point of view. It is determined by how an individual interprets or envisions something. Each one of us can express our perspectives on any given matter, whether it is the same as others or the total opposite.

I believe a person's upbringing shapes their perspective on life, as well as one's environment and experiences. There could be two different opinions or worldviews formulated by two distinct groups of people, concluded based on occurrences in their respective lives. For example, someone who grows up in a loving, two-parent, upper-middle-class environment without the same worries and trepidations as their peer who is raised in a lower-class, broken home will more likely have a different outlook on their future. The advantages of having a good support structure in the home, financial stability, and a superior educational system should foster a feeling of security that should make one comfortable enough to explore their options in life. On the other hand, having limited resources *can* cultivate a sense of hopelessness that could lead to low self-esteem resulting in a lackluster lifestyle. Now, of course, some groups are autonomous of these findings, but the fact remains, wherever you find yourself, your background will in some way, or another affect your perspective.

Recently, I was gathering statistics in regard to the community where our church is located in order to create a Needs Assessment. The purpose of the assessment was to help the church identify the needs and possible concerns of the residents, which would allow the Pastor to gain pertinent information to provide necessary programs and services to match those needs. During my research, I learned that my target area had a median household income of $38,128, which places them in the bottom six percent of the 1,675 Pennsylvania (Pa.) zip codes. [1]

---

[1] (https://pennsylvaniaometownlocatorom)

I also identified and evaluated three local schools: an elementary, middle, and high school. Without naming the institutions, the elementary school ranked 1,433rd of 1,433 Pennsylvania public elementary schools, the middle school was 797th of 797, and the high school was 536th out of 537. These schools are products of the Philadelphia school system, which has an overall rating of 473 out of 579 Pa. schools, with a 66% graduation rate for students from pre-kindergarten to 12th grade. [2] The finding of their placements had me in tears. These students were averaging between 7%-9% efficiency in math and 21%-23% in reading. This is unconscionable!

In comparison to another Pennsylvania zip code in an affluent suburban neighborhood where the median income is $136,000. Sadly, there was a vast disparity when comparing schoolshis elementary school was ranked 7th, while the middle and high schools were ranked 8th, and 33rd respectively. This suburban school system has an overall rating of 9 out of 579 Pa. schools, with a 98% graduation rate for pre-kindergarten to 12th grade students. These students were averaging between 86%-89% efficiency in math and around 96% in reading.[3] This is awesome for these young people to maintain such good grades. On the other hand, it is unacceptable that two communities, just 21 miles away from each other, would have such an inequality when it comes to education.

---

[2] (https://wwwchooldiggerom/go/PA/schools)
[3] (https://wwwchooldiggerom/go/PA/schools

In an article titled, 'Poverty's Long-Lasting Effects on Students' Education and Success' the author, Kelley Taylor, cites that in 2015, approximately 20 percent of children in the United States lived in poverty, according to the U. Census Bureau. That is to say, nearly one in five children belonged to a family composed of two adults and two children with a household income of less than $24,339 a year. This suggests that a staggering 51 percent of pre-K through 12th grade students reside in low-income households.[4] This is a sad reality that plagues many of the communities throughout the United States. I strongly believe that we can't afford the consequences that come from not equally investing in *all* of our youth's education, despite their parent's income status. There are many studies that correlate poverty with lack of education, and each claims high crime rates, juvenile delinquency, homelessness, poor health, drug abuse, and high incarceration rates.

Undoubtedly, starting behind the proverbial *8 ball* can be a difficult way to begin life for anyone. Yet, there are countless individuals who overcame tough times through hard work and sheer determination. People with various disabilities and illnesses refuse to allow their circumstances to hold them back. Even amid their situations, they were able to be victorious. How is it that some individuals can triumph over travailing issues in poor conditions and

---

[4] https://wwwnsightintodiversityom/povertys-long-lasting-effects-on-students-education-and-success.

others can't? I discovered that those who succeed despite their limitations do so because they can view themselves as victorious regardless of the unfavorable terms of their environment. Despite where they grew up or what odds may be stacked against them, they can see life according to what they desire and grab hold of a vision in which they perceive themselves as being who they want to become, doing what they long to do, and having what they truly desire.

LIFE AND DEATH ARE IN THE POWER OF YOUR TONGUE.

Whenever I address young people in particular, I always ask them to recite out loud, "There is greatness inside of me." Some say it, and some don't. To those that don't, I tell them the importance of speaking positive affirmations in their lives. If you don't speak positively about yourself, then chances are, no one else will, either. Sadly, too many of our children hear damaging expletives and phrases such as, "You're gonna end up in jail just like your father!" "You're gonna end up being a pregnant dropout just like your mother!" Unfortunately, too often, the people closest to us say the most hurtful things that become self-fulfilling prophecies that can cause a lifetime of damage. This truth was validated in an article on *CollectiveHubom* by a group of psychologists. They suggested, "For every negative encounter, there should be a minimum of five positive ones to counterbalance the effects of the first." " Not only that but when positive and negative levels are equal, bad is *still* stronger and leaves a more lasting impression." [5]

Consequently, many live out those negative images deposited in their subconscious because they never replaced them with positive ones. To support you in your journey and personal growth, I encourage you to write a few positive affirmations down on 3x5 cards, or in a journal. Then take time and recite them throughout the day to motivate and inspire yourself. Know that what you say about yourself is *exactly what you sow into yourself.* In other words, just like a farmer who plants seeds into the ground, whatever you put into the atmosphere is what's going to manifest. Therefore, deposit into your spirit declarations proclaiming that "I am wealthy" and not poor, that "I am healthy" and not sick, or that "my future is bright" in spite of my current circumstances. Do not allow your negative words to be instrumental in talking you out of your dreams. Instead, empower your words to reflect what you want in your life and who you need to become to receive it. You already have what it takes to do whatever you put your mind to do, you just have to envision yourself doing it.

---

[5] (https://collectivehubom/2017)

YOUR PERSPECTIVE CAN
DETERMINE YOUR OUTCOME

About ten years ago, I had an unforgettable incident that really challenged me. One morning, I left my home at approximately 8:15 am to go to the supermarket for some breakfast food. The ground was coated with snow, and large flakes were falling down rapidly, but I decided to take a chance and continue on to my destination. The market was about a mile and a half away, so I figured I could get there, run in, grab a few items, and get back to the house safely. To my surprise, the strangest thing occurred. I had reached about three blocks away from the house when I noticed my left front tire was flat. I then put on my spare tire and drove another four blocks to the supermarket. I ran in and got my few items, but when I returned to my car, not only was the spare tire now flat, but my right-rear tire had also gone flat! Now, having two flat tires, the snow was beginning to pile up, and visibility was close to zero. Fortunately, there was a used tire shop within walking distance. I remember carrying one tire at a time back and forth as the sharp, frigid snowflakes slammed into my face as they quickly blew through the wind. Man, it was cold!

While bearing the harsh elements, I was exhausting a lot of energy. My hands were hurting from carrying the heavy, cold steel tire rim, and the floor was becoming increasingly slippery from the fresh snow. Even though I was less than two miles from home, and people were all around me, I was beginning to feel hopeless and stranded. Knowing that what I thought was a false narrative, I quickly went into what I call 'survivor mode.' Instead of focusing on the daunting task ahead of me, I caused myself to picture myself sitting in my living room eating my breakfast (no matter what time of day) with my feet up, enjoying a game of college football. That was the thing that allowed me to make it through my ordeal. What should've taken me about 30 minutes, turned out to be a four-hour venture. Nevertheless, I had decided that no matter how long it would take me, I would make it back home *and* eat my food. I refused to allow my circumstances to determine my outcome. Once I envisioned myself in the position I wanted to be in, I gained the extra strength to persevere. What false narratives are you creating in your mind that is keeping you bound and cuffed? What are you telling yourself that is building boundaries all around you?

BUILDING WALLS WITH LIMITING BELIEFS

The great motivational speaker Les Brown once shared that he was engaged in a phone conversation with a successful individual who was trying to encourage him to go after his dreams. Despite the man's efforts, Les gave him reason after reason why he was unable to succeed. At some point, the phone went dead. Believing they were accidentally disconnected, Les called him back. The man then candidly informed Les that he deliberately hung up. When asked why, the man stated, "When you begin to argue for your limitations, you get to keep them." So, are you arguing for your limitations? Are you claiming that you want more out of life, but you are cuffing your own potential by denying yourself opportunities? Every negative word you speak against your abilities acts as a brick or cinder block that you are personally erecting one by one, which is then creating a barrier between you and the future you desire. Understand that your words have power!

BIG DREAMS, BIG RESULTS

It takes the same energy to think small as it does to think big. So, dream big and think bigger.

Daymond John,

an American Businessman, Investor, Television Personality, Author, and Motivational Speaker

To win in life, you must remove the restrictions you create in your mind and replace them with positive images of how you want your life to look. These images arise out of your passion and are not to be limited by anyone. Let your vision be as big and bold as you can see it. Don't limit yourself by making it too small because *if it is too big for you to conceive in your mind, then it will be too big for you to possess in your hand.* Your limited thinking is what restricts you from having what you desire. If your narrative is too much for you to own, then someone else will own it. If you believe you are incapable of doing it, someone else will come along and do it. My oldest daughter once told me a story of an employee who saw his boss in the parking lot washing and waxing his brand-new sports car. The employee said, "Sir, that is a beautiful sports car." The boss replied, "Thanks, young man. If you continue to work as hard as you do, then I will be able to purchase myself a brand-new one next year."

Aren't you tired of seeing others living the dreams you once imagined? Can you see yourself uncuffed from fear, past failures, and self-doubt? If you want to start living a life of peace and prosperity, you must use your faith to tear down the mental walls of restriction that keep you from the successful life you desire. Concentrate on what you are passionate about and what you can see yourself doing in the future. Don't worry about *how* you're going to do it, just focus on what you do best, and invest as much time and energy in developing your skills. I heard Jim Rohn once say, "Learn to work harder on yourself than you do on your job. If you work hard on your job, you can make a living, but if you work hard on yourself, you'll make a fortune." Think big. Put your ideas on paper and go over them repeatedly so you can get them embedded into your mind. What you study longest becomes the strongest and will dominate your thoughts, and your thoughts will eventually become actions.

SUCCESS BEGINS IN THE MIND

Imagination is everything. It is the preview of life's coming attractions.

Albert Einstein,

A German-born Theoretical Physicist.

It is safe to say that the great former Dallas Cowboys running back, Emmitt Smith (who was a 3-time Super Bowl™ winner and the Most Valuable Player of Super Bowl XXVIII, as well as the overall MVP of the 1992 season) knows a little something about winning. Emmitt once said, "For me, winning is not something that happens suddenly on the field when the whistle blows and the crowds roar. Winning is something that builds physically and mentally every day that you train and every night that you dream."

In other words, success is *NOT* something that comes upon you. It gives birth inside of your thought patterns that have been playing over and over again in your head.

Long before Emmitt arrived in Dallas and set the all-time NFL™ rushing record of 18,355 yards in 15 seasons, he saw himself crossing the goal line hundreds of times while day-dreaming as a little boy growing up in Pensacola, Florida. You probably will not find anyone who knew Emmitt as a child that would be surprised by his success. Everything he imagined himself doing, he accomplished throughout his illustrious career.

DON'T LOSE SIGHT OF YOUR DREAMS

There are countless examples of athletes, entertainers, and other successful people who achieved their success in different professions, but one thing they all have in common is that at some point they imagined themselves performing in their area of expertise before it manifested in their lives. For instance, Stefani Joanne Angelina Germanotta, who is known as Lady Gaga, says that before becoming a world-renown singer and songwriter, her childhood dream was to become an actress. At age 19, she went to acting school but admits she was not good at auditioning. But despite this setback, she decided to put her aspirations for acting on hold and shifted her focus to a career in music. As a teenager, she worked as a waitress to fund her music career, performed at *open mic nights* at clubs and bars, and acted in school plays.[6]

---

[6] https://wwwfeom/efe/english/entertainment/lady-gaga

Today, Lady Gaga is a well-known singer and actress. Since 2005 until now, she has amassed an astounding total of 358 awards out of 842 nominations for music and acting. She also has a net worth of $320 million. Most when the name Lady Gaga is mentioned will think of her for her fame as a singer, but being a world-renowned singer alone was not fulfilling for her. Lady Gaga's story should teach us not to settle but always keep our sights on what we are passionate about. She has now gone from appearing in minor acting roles to starring in major films. She also became the first female artist to win all five big awards in 2019 when she won an Oscar®, Golden Globe™, Grammy, British Academy of Film, Television (BAFTA™), and a Critic's Choice Award™.

For you, it might not be football, singing, or acting, but whatever your gift is, frame in your mind that success is possible. Envision yourself daily managing your dream business, accepting that prestigious award, and signing that multi-million-dollar contract. Whatever you desire to become, be clear about why it is important to you, and go for it!

Perspective is the first of the five fundamental principles that will help you uncuff your potential. The very essence of the word means *to see through or forward.* You need to have a positive perspective in order to see yourself going above and beyond your circumstances. Perspective helps you to become certain about what you want and in what direction to go.

CHAPTER II

WALKING WITH CERTAINTY

New Thoughts, New Results,
New Perspectives

*Clarity and simplicity are the antidotes to
complexity and uncertainty.*

General George Casey Retired
*four-star general who served as the 36th Chief of Staff of the
United States Army.*

Now that you have broadened your perspective and perceive things from another vantage point, the path to your desires should be more apparent. It is vitally important to be willing to expand your vision beyond your present position, if not, it would be rather challenging to elevate to a higher level. Albert Einstein once said, "We cannot solve our problems with the same thinking we used when we created them." Therefore, in order to break out of those limitations that have kept you from getting what you want, you must be willing to forego beliefs that led you to the place you claim you no longer want to be.

YOU MUST SEE YOURSELF WINNING!

If you don't see yourself as a winner,
then you cannot perform as a winner.

Zig Ziglar,
An American author, salesman, and motivational speaker.

No athlete puts in grueling hours by punishing their body in the gym, putting in extra reps of practice, or playing through nagging injuries, only to take the playing field of their respective sport expecting to lose the game. We all know that losing is always a possibility in life, but no one consciously enters into the arena of life with a mindset of failing. Michael Jordan never took a shot expecting to miss. With every crushing swing of her tennis racket, Serena Williams always expected to hit the ball past her oppo-nent. And the great Hall of Fame™ baseball player known as "Mr. October," Reggie Jackson, approached the plate every time with the expectation of hitting a home run. Having a winner's perspective, like these great athletes who were all once champions, will break the mindset of uncertainty. Those who routinely approach challenges in life pessimistically tend to wander through life, not hoping to lose. You cannot win in this world if you allow your thoughts of victory to be overshadowed by feelings of failure. It is imperative to expand your horizons because you can never go beyond where you place your limitations. Wherever you set your boundaries is the very place your growth stops. Whether it's education, a career, or relationships, success can only go as far as you will allow.

HOW TO EXPAND BEYOND YOUR CIRCUMSTANCES

One sunny afternoon, I was sitting inside my car in a convenience store's parking lot when I noticed a gentleman walking by hastily. The mildly disheveled, middle-aged man abruptly stopped, reached into the trash bin, found a tattered piece of cardboard, whipped out a marker, and began writing a message on the front of it. No sooner than he finished writing, he quickly walked from the parking lot to the northwest corner of the boulevard. There he held up his sign, and within minutes, several motorists handed him money from their cars while idling at the traffic light. I watched this continue to unfold for about 15 minutes as I sat eating my sandwich. I was fascinated by the number of cars that stopped and gave this man money. I thought to myself, *This was brilliant!* Here is a man who appeared to be down on his luck and probably used his only resources and wrote his story. He believed in whatever he wrote enough that it would bring him a return that would improve his circumstances.

IS YOUR GLASS HALF EMPTY OR HALF FULL?

Sadly, there is probably someone else on the other side of town with the same set of circumstances and resources, but they see their situation from a totally different perspective. From a glass- half empty approach, their story accentuates everything that is seemingly wrong, giving credit to issues such as a bad divorce, the loss of a job, or a series of unforeseeable failures. And unlike the first man with the half-full approach, who used his resources to overcome his current state of affairs, the other man uses his resources to tell a narrative of hopelessness, lack, and misery. The end result: one man eats and lives to see another day, while the next man starves to death from a diet filled with negative thoughts and lowly feelings about himself. Ask yourself, am I the glass-half-full, or half-empty type? Am I blaming others for my shortcomings, or am I taking responsibility for where I am? Whatever your answer is, remember that you are the sum total of the decisions you make.

THEY BOTH EXIST ACCORDING TO YOUR THOUGHTS

In life, there are always two sides that are both existing at the same time. For example, there is hot and cold, light and darkness, good and bad; they are all polar opposites of each other, but they're present and available for all to experience. Although they are distinctly different, together, they co-exist in our world. Despite the polarity between heads and tails, only one side of the coin is revealed when it is flipped. Whether it always seems to land on heads, and you chose tails or vice versa, you cannot deny the existence of the other. The same principle applies to wealth and poverty. They are drastically different but dwell in the same realm of possibilities. Despite a person's circumstances, they have the propensity to obtain anything they want. The choice is yours.

The man I encountered in the store lot did not limit himself to his environment where lack existed. Instead, he moved away from scarcity and used his resources to get what he needed. On the other hand, others choose to focus on their circumstances and what they don't have so much that they never get a glimpse at what is possible, although it's only on the other side of the coin. No one gets to choose their coin in life, but you can choose which side you will be on.

KEEP YOUR EYES ON THE PRIZE

Adversity causes some men to break,
others to break records.

William Arthur Ward

An American motivational writer

When you have been conditioned to see yourself a particular way for a substantial period of time, breaking that perspective can be difficult to do. Change is never easy, but it is absolutely necessary if you no longer want to remain in the state that you're in. One way to do so is by imagining yourself out of the situation while you're still in it. I recall going through a bad breakup and moving from my home into a very modest, one-bedroom apartment. In order to be able to afford the apartment, I had to downsize from a new car to a much older vehicle. I could not afford to buy new furniture, but I was blessed by friends and family, as well as grabbing some household items that my new neighbors had discarded. I was given two 19-inch color televisions (tv), and the best of them had a bad picture tube that was obviously approaching its final days. The left side of the tv screen was a burgundy color, and the right side was light green *(I can laugh about this now.)*. I struggled for three years to pay the rent while living paycheck to paycheck. Despite those tough times, I never lost sight of my dream of living in a beautiful four-bedroom, two-door garage, three bathrooms, a huge, finished basement, and a deck. I also saw myself driving a nice new car and having a beautiful, loving wife to enjoy life together.

It took hard work, faith, and determination to move from a life of lack to a lifestyle I saw myself capable of living. For this to happen, I had to redefine my perspective, set goals, and take action *(I'll discuss planning and goal setting in more detail in chapters 9 & 10)*. As a result, the things that I prayed for during my trying times have come true. Today I have exactly what I dreamed of. I have a beautiful home in the suburbs with all of the amenities, a nice new luxury vehicle, and, most importantly, my lovely wife. I'm not stating my accomplishments to boast, but to stress the importance of never losing sight of your dreams, no matter how difficult things may become for you. I encourage you to take your eyes off your problems so they do not restrain you from achieving what you wish for. Instead, use those tough times to uncuff the potential that lies within. And remember;

"Tough times do not come to stay, they come to pass."

-Les Brown

TURN YOUR TRAGEDY INTO TRIUMPH

Every worthwhile accomplishment,
big or little, has its stages of
drudgery and triumph: a beginning,
a struggle, and a victory.

Mahatma Gandhi,

An Indian lawyer, anti-colonial
nationalist, and political ethicist.

One of my favorite stories to tell is about a virtually unknown, uncelebrated American hero, Bridget "Biddy" Mason, who was born into slavery in Hancock, Georgia, in 1818 (Other accounts list her birthplace as Hancock, Mississippi). In 1840, Biddy was sold, or as some say, she was given to enslaver Robert Mayes Smith and his wife as a wedding present in Mississippi. Despite the apparent atrocities that were associated with being a slave, Biddy had to endure the unthinkable. When her owner decided to move from Mississippi to Salt Lake Valley, UT, on a seven-year journey, 30 year-old Mason walked 1,700 miles behind a 300-wagon caravan to their new home.

During this grueling journey, some of her responsibilities included cooking the meals, herding the cattle, serving as a midwife, and taking care of her three young daughters, including an infant. But do not cry for Biddy! Before her death in 1881 in Los Angeles, although she was illiterate, Biddy obtained her freedom and became a real estate mogul and philanthropist. At her death in 1891, Biddy Mason's wealth was approximately $300,000, or about $7,000,000 in today's dollars. More impressively, the land she owned in downtown Los Angeles is now worth hundreds of millions. Through it all, she achieved financial success that enabled her to support her extended family for generations. It is people like Biddy who took the harshest of times and still found a way to fulfill their destiny.

Then there is 28-year-old Shareif "Reef" Hall, who saw his life dramatically changed at the tender age of four. On a typical November day in Philadelphia, PA, the most unimaginable and horrifying event took place while exiting the subway station with his mother. Shareif's right foot was somehow severed in the faulty escalator he and his mother were exiting. At such an early age, he faced a dilemma that could physically and emotionally scar him for life.

For some time, the young man struggled with accepting his injury, and as you could imagine, it was difficult for a child to be seen out in public as being different. Therefore, he hid his leg as much as possible. But over time, he began to recognize that the loss of a foot did not define him, and he was determined to turn his tragedy into triumph! Today, he is celebrating his disability as a model by using his prosthetic leg as a billboard to display art to promote products for various businesses. He is also a part of other business ventures and a bonafide success story, demonstrating that you *can* live out your passion and overcome anything once you change your perspective.

In your own life, I'm sure you can speak about some tragedies that occurred that rocked your world. One thing is for sure, trials don't just come once, but they show up time after time in various ways. That's why I believe that life is too precious to live with uncertainty and without enjoyment. Having a firm perspective of who you are and what you want will help free you from a mindset that keeps you in bondage. I love this quote from Pastor Steven Furtick of Charlotte, NC, *Your perspective will either become your passport or your penitentiary.* This is so true. How you view yourself is a choice, and that choice will shape the outcome of your life. Since you have a choice, choose to see yourself successful, living the life you desire, even if you're not currently where you want to be.

CHAPTER III

UNLEASH YOUR PASSION

*Passion is energy. Feel the
power that comes from focusing
on what excites you.*

Oprah Winfrey

*An American talk show host, television producer, actress,
author, and philanthropist.*

What is Passion? Passion is that inescapable feeling that you go to sleep thinking about, and it is still on your mind when you wake up. No, I am not talking about lust or physical passion, but something very powerful that God has placed in each one of us. It is that feeling you get when performing what you are gifted to do that makes you feel you were born to do it. I get that feeling whenever I speak on stage, teach in a classroom, or just encourage someone. What is something you do that you feel you're best at and that gives you your greatest fulfillment? Is it working with children and seeing them happy, or cooking delicious meals and watching others enjoy their food?

Some people do not believe they have purpose, skills, or talents, but I beg to differ. It is not that God skipped over anyone when handing out gifts and abilities; it's just we were all blessed differently. Like any manufacturer, God desires to bring the best out in all of us. He endowed us with the appropriate tools to thrive in our talents to ensure our success. For some, it is the wonderful ability to sing, and for others, the grace to paint an award-winning portrait. Whatever that may be it is your assignment to discover it. And once you identify what you are passionate about, then you can find your purpose.

GROWTH THROUGH YOUR FAITH

"Do not despise these small beginnings, for the Lord rejoices to see the work begin."

The Bible, Zechariah 4:10, New Living Translation

One reason why some people do not start working in their passion is because they fear they do not have enough resources to do the work. But there are several references in the bible that show the success you can have with just a little when you put your faith in it. Remember that Jesus, with only two fish and five loaves of bread, he fed 5,000 people *(Mattew 14:13-21)* , or when Gideon defeated thousands of men after he reduced his army from 22,000 men to just 300 *(Judges chapter 7)*. What are you allowing to hold you back from doing something you desire to do? God is willing to help fulfill the passion that is in your heart. One Father's Day evening in 1996, Pastor Brian Jenkins and his wife attended a play in downtown Philadelphia, Pa. As they exited the historical Merriam Theater, they encountered a man who appeared to be homeless. All the other patrons walked by the man whose hair was long and unkept. He wore pants that were stained and held up by a rope, and a make-shift shirt from a torn blanket that exposed his meatless ribs. Unlike everyone else who kept walking by, the Jenkins stopped and learned that the man's name was Mr. Jones. All they had left to offer him was forty-cents and an apology for not being able to do more. His reply was *"But you considered me..."* His reply is what sparked the mission and ministry now known as, "Chosen 300 Ministries, Inc.

The next week, the Jenkins prepared bagged lunches at their home which shortly outgrew their ability to provide the meals on their own. Today, over 115 religious organizations, companies and community groups distribute over 150,000 full course meals throughout the Philadelphia region. Chosen 300 Ministries also provides more than 500,000 pounds of food and humanitarian aid in 24 locations across 9 countries. Brian never saw Mr. Jones again, but stated, *"I see the smile he had on his face that night every time I see the smile of another homeless person we reach."* Pastor Jenkins did not allow only having forty-cents to stop him from following his passion. And I believe there is something God has for you to do as well, but you have to see the big outcomes you can achieve while you still only have little.

WHAT FITS YOU DOESN'T NECESSARILY FIT ME

When you finally begin to operate in your passion, you will know it, even when others will not understand. "Why are you accepting less money?" "Why did she turn down the promotion?" "That does not make sense for him to leave that great position." As soon as you come to understand your purpose, the sooner you can be released from the control of others' ideas and opinions. What God has for you is exclusively for you, and what He designed for me is for me. My purpose in life might not fit in your world, and vice versa.

One of the greatest men recorded in antiquity was King David. During a period in his life as a young shepherd boy, David was going into battle against his oversized opponent, Goliath. King Saul and the Israelite soldiers feared the giant Philistine and trembled at the sound of his voice as he hurled insults against the God of Israel. Unwilling to fight, King Saul tried to clothe David in his war clothes.

In the Bible it says, *Samuel 17:38-39 (NKJV)*

38), *So Saul clothed David with his armor, and he put a bronze helmet on his head; he also covered him with a coat of mail.*

39), *David fastened his sword to his armor and tried to walk, for he had not tested them. And David said to Saul, "I cannot walk with these, for I have not tested them." So, David took them off."* — Sometimes, we allow others to put expectations on us that were not designed for our lives. They tell you to go to school and get an education to get a good job or go into 'this or that' field of study because that is where the money is. For these reasons, many people are living frustrated, unfulfilled lives because they are stuck in dead-end careers, failing marriages, and financial hardships. Following the ideas of others and not listening to your heart can leave you feeling like a square peg stuffed inside a round hole; stuck and clueless because you climbed into somebody else's idea for your life instead of following your heart. Always remember, "Working hard for something you don't care for is called stress, but working hard for something you love is called passion."

GO WITH WHAT YOU GOT

King David attributed any success he experienced to God alone. Although he was just a young shepherd, he was fearless, ready to endure an epic battle against someone much larger and more experienced than him. Nevertheless, this was not David's first fight, and he was not about to back down.

I Samuel 17:33-37a (NKJV) says,

33) And Saul said to David, You are not able to go against this Philistine to fight with him; for you are a youth, and he's a man of war from his youth.

34) But David said to Saul, "Your servant used to keep his father's sheep, and when a lion or a bear came and took a lamb out of the flock, 35) I went out after it and struck it, and delivered the lamb from its mouth; and when it arose against me, I caught it by its beard and struck and killed it.

36) Your servant has killed both lion and bear; and this Philistine (Goliath) will be like one of them, seeing he has defied the armies of the living God.

37) Moreover, David said, "The Lord, who delivered me from the paws of the lion and the paw of the bear. He will deliver me from the hand of this Philistine."

Saul tries to point out to David all of the odds that were against him. Ignoring the odds, David reminded himself of what God provided for him in the past, and that He can do the same for him in this situation as well. Saul wanted David to see how big the problem was, but instead, David magnified how big his God was! And as a result, David respectfully rejected Saul's proposal and refused to wear his armor to battle. Instead, the audacious youth went into combat against Goliath, with a slingshot and five smooth stones he found in a brook. With this alone, he was able to slay the Philistine giant. Whatever your gift is, it does not have to be as flashy or as extravagant as what someone else has. You may not have a master's degree hanging over your fireplace, or a bunch of letters behind your last name. You just have to believe in yourself and be proficient with what you have, and use it to conquer whatever life throws your way.

BE PASSIONATE ABOUT YOUR LIFE (YOU ONLY GET ONE)

A life without passion is not living;
It is merely existing.

Leo Buscaglia

An American Author, Motivational Speaker, and Professor
known as "Dr. Love."

One of my favorite success stories to tell is that of the late Alexandra "Alex" Scott. Alex is the founder of the popularly known, Alex's Lemonade Stand, which is a charitable foundation for pediatric cancer patients. Shortly before her first birthday, Alex was diagnosed with neuroblastoma, a type of childhood cancer. Her doctors informed Alex's parents that if she beat her cancer, it was doubtful that she would ever walk again. When she was just four years old, Alex told her mother that once released from the hospital; she wanted to open a lemonade stand so that she could give doctors money to help other children who have cancer.

Later that year, she held her first lemonade stand and raised an astounding $2,000 in her front yard for 'her hospital.' By the time of her death in 2004, Alex had raised $1 million and inspired a legacy of hope and cures for childhood cancer. How is it, you ask, that a child dying of cancer at the tender age of eight years old could be a success story?

Although this story is a definite tear-jerker and granted, she had a bright future ahead of her. In eight years, Alex was able to accomplish what most adults are unwilling to do. Despite the odds and obstacles surrounding her health, she discovered her purpose for existing and followed her passion for helping save others.

I hope stories like this inspire you to follow your passion. As you see, a long life is not promised, but what you do with your time is what matters most. It's been said that "Most people die at age 25, and are buried at age 65." This means that many people stop living their lives for personal fulfillment but instead, they put all their energy into working hard to pay their bills and take care of their families. Unfortunately, they do not take any time for themselves while life is quickly passing them by. You only have one life, live it unapologetically to its fullest.

NEVER GIVE UP ON YOUR DREAMS

For those of you who feel lost with no direction, you may simply need to reevaluate where you are in life and where you want your life to be. Commonly, people live despondently while subscribing to the notion that because they have been going a particular way for so long, there is no other way to proceed. Over the years, I have listened to many long-tenured fellow police officers who expressed difficulty seeing themselves or their peers doing any type of work that is not associated with law enforcement. Talk of doing anything other than being a cop breeds resistance. Even though there is a great consensus amongst police officers that those in the law enforcement profession are grossly underappreciated and are gradually being stripped of their ability to do their job. Nevertheless, many officers would rather persevere and continue to work well into their sixties and even seventies with the sole purpose of collecting a fat monthly pension check. Sadly, some officers get so close to retiring but never get a chance to enjoy it. Just recently, in western Pennsylvania, an officer was shot to death inside the suspect's home on a domestic call. He was 67 years old and less than a week from retiring. I also lost a buddy whom I had known my entire career, who had his sights on retirement but died of Covid-19 at the age of 59.

In life, it's not that you lack the ability to choose another path in life or are not capable of achieving your goals. Sometimes you have to be willing to take chances and not be afraid to pivot *out of one thing into another*. For instance, at age 51, with close to 28 years in law enforcement, and a primarily comfortable, plainclothes, desk job, I went to work one Friday morning, sat at my desk, and decided I was done. I announced to my captain that this was my last day and that I was retiring. This took him and all of my colleagues by total surprise. Even though this was a huge step for me, especially because I was not exactly sure what the next phase of my life would look like, I can honestly tell you that I did not have one ounce of fear or doubt that I was making the right decision.

Oftentimes, while working for an employer, you become so inundated and bogged down with all kinds of issues and never get an opportunity to focus on what you were truly called to do. When I made my decision, some applauded me and even began to consider retiring themselves, while others said I was foolish for retiring at such a young age. As I earlier mentioned, although Saul suggested that David put on his armor to fight Goliath, David understood his position in life and wisely rejected his request. There will always be a "Saul" in your life who will attempt to transfer their limitations onto you and expect you to wear them as your own. And, because people who have these limitations are fearful and not confident to step out on faith or take risks, they will try to convince you to either choose the safest route or return unsatisfied to live below your means, standing on the sidelines of life.

DO NOT ALLOW ANYONE TO QUENCH YOUR PASSION

Twenty years from now you will be more disappointed by the things you didn't do than by the ones you did do.

Mark Twain,

An American Writer, Humorist, Entrepreneur, Publisher, and Lecturer.

I'm sure we have all heard the saying, "Why put off tomorrow what you can do today?" Many caring parents have been known to put off their dreams and aspirations to accommodate their children. And on the flip side, many children do something other than what they desire in an attempt to please their parents. Often, both parents and children sacrifice their dreams to live vicariously through the other or worse, persuade one another to do something other than go after their personal desires

There was a man by the name of Matt Groening who had a great passion for drawing at a young age. As the son of a prominent filmmaker, advertiser, writer, and cartoonist, Matt had a vivid imagination and desired to follow in his father's footsteps. He also drew further inspiration after watching the animation movie *101 Dalmatians*™ and from his admiration of cartoonist Charles Monroe Schulz, who was known for his comic creation 'Peanuts.' Later, in college, Groening became the editor for his school's newspaper, and after graduating, he headed to Los Angeles with the idea of pursuing a writing career. He found some work along those lines in the writing industry, whipping up slogans for horror movies, but also took on a series of jobs that included chauffeur, dishwasher, and record store clerk to make a living. Groening also created a comic book titled "Life in Hell," that he stapled together and mailed to friends and family back in Portland. He attempted to sell his books from his record store.

Despite his hard work and tenacity, Groening's own father told Matt that his drawing skills were so bad he'd never be able to make a living as a cartoonist. Believing his dad, he sought to make a living through writing only, but by then, the Life in Hell comic had already been noticed as it was featured weekly in the L. Reader Newspaper." Then in 1987, Groening got the chance of a lifetime. He had been called to pitch a series of short, animated cartoons based on his comic strip "Life in Hell" for the half-hour "Tracey Ullman Show." Instead, while he was waiting in the lobby of producer James L. Brooks' office, he decided to create a new set of characters. Groening elected to name the characters after members of his own family: his parents, Homer and Marge (Margaret or Marjorie in full), and his younger sisters, Lisa and Margaret (Maggie). Not wanting to be too obvious to name a character after himself, he chose the name "Bart," an anagram of brat.

After appearing for three seasons on The Tracey Ullman Show, the Simpson family got their own Fox series, debuting on December 17, 1989. In 1990 The Simpsons won the first of its more than 20 Emmy Awards, and in 2009 it became the longest-running prime-time series in American television history. And for the young Matt Groening, who was told by his father he would never make a living as a cartoonist, is now worth $500 million! What if he would have listened to his father instead of following his passion? How much different would his life be today if he had allowed someone else to dictate what career to pursue? I urge you to unleash your own passion! Free yourself of the opinions of others and do what makes you feel good inside.

You have a passion inside of you that can no longer be hidden. There are people around you and throughout the world who can benefit from the things you have to offer. Right now, there is a burning desire for you to become the person you have always envisioned yourself being. That person already exists, but *you* must declare that the time is now for that person inside you to be released. Life is *too* short and precious to waste. So, stop waiting to be happy. Stop waiting for your circumstances to change and decide today that you will become so passionate about your life that nothing will stand in your way from doing what you want to do. "There is no passion to be found playing small – in settling for a life that is less than the one you are capable of living." – *(Nelson Mandela)* You only get one life to live, so why not live it to the fullest by letting your passion lead you? Don't let others decide for you. They don't know what stirs you up on the inside, only you do. So again, only do what drives you, and do whatever your assignment is for your life with great passion and honor.

CHAPTER IV

DO WHAT YOU ARE PASSIONATE ABOUT

If you do what you love, you'll never work a day in your life.

Marc Anthony

Singer and Songwriter

I believe that the average person is working in a particular industry, not because they love what they do, but
because that is the job in which they settled. Don't get me
wrong, there is nothing wrong with working in any job, but
hopefully, it is a position that gives you great fulfillment.
I worked as a police officer for 29 years, and in the midst
of the danger, gory sights, and unfavorable assignments,
I still found great satisfaction in helping people. There
may be times when you do have to take a job or even a
second job just to feed your family. It may require you to do

something that you are not particularly passionate about or does not align with your core values. If that is the case, then I suggest that you do what you have to do to supply your needs but never lose sight of your dreams.

I once read a book entitled, *Caught Between A Dream And a Job: How to Leave the 9-to-5 Behind and Step Into the Life You've Always Wanted* by author and motivational speaker Delatorro McNeal. He expressed that he became a professor at his alma mater, Florida State University (FSU) soon after he graduated. It was a job he enjoyed, but he was passionate about his dream of becoming a motivational speaker. So, Delatorro worked out a deal with the FSU that allowed him to continue to work his full-time hours for four days a week, instead of five days. With the extra day off, he used his additional time to focus on his dream job, which eventually earned him more income than his job as a professor. As an author, he encourages the readers of his book to systematically move from *job living to dream living,* and *to do what they love to do*—and get paid to do it. This is great for those who have a desire to someday work for themselves. This may not be everyone's story, but I would be willing to bet that most people are not working their dream jobs.

The real estate tycoon and best-selling author Robert Kiyosaki once quoted, "Workers work hard enough to not be fired, and owners pay just enough so that workers won't quit." Although this statement may be a bit facetious, if you find yourself working a job you are not passionate about, I suggest you invest in yourself by increasing your skills and value. If you give your job eight or more hours a day, forty-plus hours a week, then it is equally important to devote ample time to your own personal development as you work to create a lifestyle that is centered around your passion.

PASSION IS AN INSIDE JOB

I can recall a time during my career as a police officer when I was out patrolling my beat and came across a young man just standing out at the corner of a street where drug dealing and various crimes took place. I decided to engage him in a conversation, and when I asked what he was doing out there, he replied, "Nothing." Selling drugs, robbing, and shooting people were obviously concerning, but doing *nothing* was also troubling to me. I would watch day-after-day, countless amounts of people throughout the community remaining idle, seemingly without hope. I asked the young man, who could not have been more than 20 years old, "What do you like to do?" He remained silent, not protesting the question, but he appeared to be taken aback by my inquiry. He eventually answered me with his head down as if he were ashamed, "I don't know. No one has ever asked me that before."

It seems that this is a question we all should be able to answer, but many can't. I believe that it is difficult for some to resolve in their minds because they believe the answer is outside of them. They think what they are passionate about must be found if searched for on Google™ or Instagram™. Whatever it is they love to do must first meet society's standards and produce six figures to be accepted. Many police officers, like myself, joined law enforcement in hopes of helping people and making communities safe. I always say that doctors, lawyers, nurses, and other service-oriented careers are merely different vehicles for helping people, and it is the passion behind the profession that is simply the common thread.

One person I met in my department several years ago was Detective Terri J. Brown. She was a very kind, humble, soft-spoken person who was always happy to help others. For a person with such a positive demeanor, I was surprised to hear she had a rough childhood. She shared with me that she became a juvenile delinquent at age 13, and homeless by age 16. Having absolutely nothing, Terri was able to turn her life around through sheer determination to succeed. With the help of mentors, Terri learned everything she could pertaining to real estate and became an owner of multiple investment properties and the founder of several companies by her early 30s.

This is more than just a story about financial success, it

is a story about passion. What I love most about Terri's story is her heartfelt desire to help others avoid the pitfalls she encountered in her youth. Today, she is a minister, a successful real estate investor, and the proud owner of Built to Last, LLC, a community development company. Her mantra is, *All things are possible for them that believe*. First, as a police officer and later as a detective, Terri had a first-hand account of the needs of people who, for decades, have been disenfranchised and suffered systemic racism. Nevertheless, she uses her personal development and real estate expertise to bring about change by helping create financial freedom and homeownership. Terri recently retired from the police department and continues to pursue her passion full-time to help others to grow and succeed.

Terri's rise from homelessness to providing homes to others through real estate investing is a testament to how your passion can lead you into your life's work. It was her back story that helped fuel her zeal for helping others. Combining her experiences and resources from her career in law enforcement with her enthusiasm to change lives, Terri created a wonderful living for herself and her family, as well as making a difference in the lives of many.

BE LED BY YOUR PASSIONS, NOT YOUR EMOTIONS

For as long as I can remember, I have always been a busy person. Whether it was playing sports as a youngster or picking up an extra shift on the job. Friends and family would always say, "Man, you are always busy." But over time, I would soon learn that being busy does not necessarily translate to being productive.

Over the past few years, I unwisely took on greater responsibilities and challenges that were not my own. Every time someone started a ministry or some sort of project, out of loyalty, I would partner with them simply upon their request. Soon after, I would regret not declining their invitations. Because of my inability to say no, often, I found myself overwhelmed and faced with the reality of taking care of the needs of my family, serving God's people, attending to work obligations and managing whatever little time I had left for myself.

After a much-needed self-assessment, I unapologetically let go of the many stresses I had committed to. I abruptly stopped working on other folks' dreams and bright ideas. I was inspired by a quote that helped solidify my decision to free myself from other people's agendas. *If you don't build your dreams, someone will hire you to help build theirs.* From that moment, I began to do a *spiritual cleansing* by reevaluating what serves me well and what is exhausting my energy and keeping me from reaching my potential. It was like reprogramming a computer and cleaning out the spam, junk mail, cookies, and all those open apps that keep it from operating efficiently.

However, there's nothing wrong with helping others, but you must discern when to do so and when to decline. I came to accept that it is okay to say no. As a matter of fact, "NO" is a complete sentence with a period (.) at the end and in some cases, an exclamation mark (!). It is very important to exercise self-care by looking out for your well-being and saying yes or no to what fits best for you.

DON'T BE A PEOPLE PLEASER

As I said previously, there is nothing wrong with helping people, but you must establish boundaries. If you are on a quest to live a gratifying life, you must begin to learn to consider your needs first. Just as in finances; if you do not include paying yourself first in your budget then you won't have anything left to invest for you. The same goes for life. You can do many things for everyone else, but you have to do more for yourself. Whenever I address police recruits before their graduation, I tell them that, "Being a police officer is like being a bank account, everyone makes withdrawals and no deposits, leaving you insufficient."

Carrying out your duties is a must, but you cannot afford to give your job *all* of your time.

Many years ago, when I was in the Police Academy, I was the driver for several people. In the morning, I would pick up my cousin and one of my classmates, and we all drove in together to training. After class, I would also drop them off at their homes. One particular day, I dropped off my nephew first, my classmate, then my cousin, and before I could make it home, I ran out of gas. This was an example of my life; sometimes, I would find myself doing so much that I never realized I was running out of gas. I was pleasing everyone else but myself. I had nothing reserved for myself.

Again, there is nothing wrong with helping people. I actually get great satisfaction when assisting others. But there is a danger to being a *people pleaser*. It can be physically and mentally taxing and cause you to feel empty and overwhelmed. According to *WebMD™*, "People pleasers may spend so much time trying to please others that they don't know what to do with themselves if there's no one asking them for something."[7] This can definitely be damaging to one's self-esteem.

There was a time I found that to be true in my life. I realized that I would go out of my way to please others so much that, at times I would neglect my own needs. If you asked

---

[7] (https://wwwebmdom/mental-health/what-is-a-people-pleaser)

me to be there, without hesitation, I was there. My schedule mainly consisted of me taking care of the needs of people and barely anything gratifying for myself. There would be no hobbies or *me-time* checked off of my to-do list. I recently read a quote that absolutely nailed it! "You are not required to set yourself on fire to keep others warm." *(Unknown source)* This is so true. If all of your energy is exhausted by you fulfilling everyone else's needs and *not your own,* then while you're making everyone else happy, you will become frustrated and miserable. Does this sound like you? Until you learn that it is alright to take care of yourself first, and then others, you will never be able to reach your full potential and enjoy the life you deserve.

PASSION: THE ANSWER TO YOUR PURPOSE

If you can't figure out your purpose, figure out your passion. For your passion will lead you right into your purpose.

Bishop Thomas Dexter Jakes Sr. (T. Jakes)

Pastor, Author, and Filmmaker

Your life needs to be filled with passion, your own passion. Not with what someone else is great at or what people influence you to do. Be filled with what gives you the most fulfillment when you do it. This is vital because you only get one chance at life. Therefore, why not live it to its fullest? Why not live your life on your terms and do the things that make you feel good about yourself? When you allow your passion to flow, it leads you to discover your purpose. I believe God designed it that way to make it easy to find, and when you connect your passion with your potential, your purpose becomes more apparent.

For example, British author and philanthropist Joanne "J." Rowling, while growing up in Gloucestershire, England, always knew she wanted to be an author. From as early as age five, she was extremely passionate about writing, and she would constantly write and tell stories to her younger sister, Dianne. Rowling said in a speech at her 2008 Harvard University commencement that she was convinced at an early age that the only thing she ever wanted to do was write novels. As a result of following her passion, J. Rowling would go on to create the world-famous fictional character Harry Potter™ through her seven-book series of novels she wrote. Also, Warner Bros™. produced eight Harry Potter films, and together with the novels, they had a combined gross of more than $15 billion. Today, Rowling is worth a whopping $1 billion. Following your passion can be worthwhile.

What sets her apart from many who still struggle to find their purpose is that she remained locked into that same passion from her youth. You, too, can discover your greatness. Find out what you are called to do by exploring what you're passionate about. Stop settling for things you don't like and focus on what you enjoy. Think of something if you did, the world would become a better place. Now take a moment and find a quiet place to collect your thoughts, and write down some things you are passionate about. Don't make a list of chores, but something you would love to do.

1. _____

2. _____

3. _____

4. _____

5. _____

Now that you have written down what you are passionate about, read it over daily to remind yourself of what you want to do. Then imagine yourself doing exactly what you love to do over and over again until it becomes a reality. Remember what I said in Chapter 1, "your perspective frames your world and can determine your outcome." In a world that is at times busy and ever-changing, it can be easy to lose sight of your passion. This is why it is extremely important to concentrate on the things you desire. In addition to keeping a vision of your passion, begin to take action by using the power you have inside. This is your potential. Whatever you are passionate about achieving, you already have the potential to accomplish it.

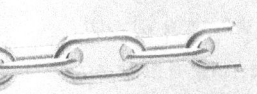 

CHAPTER V

TAP INTO YOUR POTENTIAL

There is no heavier burden than an unfulfilled potential.

Charles Schulz,

An American Cartoonist

Up to now we have talked about perspective and passion, two things that are vital to helping you *uncuff your potential.* Having the ability to see yourself living a successful life and being passionate about your future leads to the next key: *potential.*

What is Potential? Potential is the unused or unrealized ability that we all possess. I believe that with God's divine purpose for our existence, each of us has the potential to become or the capability to produce something great. We all have a power within us and the ability to create.

Unfortunately, that power often goes undiscovered or unutilized. One of the reasons I am so passionate about helping troubled youth is because I have faith that if they knew their purpose and realized the potential they possess, their lives would be impacted powerfully. When you know your purpose (what you were born to do) and understand the strengths you possess (your potential), then you'll know where to place your focus. Potential is not what you have already done. It is not what you have used up—rather, the potential is what you still have left in the tank.

One of my favorite people on the planet is the great Shaquille O'Neal. Although *"Shaq"* is most known for his dominant 19- year NBA™ career in which he played for (6) teams and is currently considered one of the greatest players in league history, I purposely did not refer to him as "the great basketball player, Shaquille O'Neal," because he is so much more.

As a retired professional basketball player, Shaq is most noted for his shenanigans as a sports analyst on the television program "Inside the NBA™" on TNT™. In addition to a Hall of Fame career, which includes receiving Rookie of the Year honors in the 1992–1993 season, (4) NBA™ titles, (15) All-Star game selections, (3) All-Star Game MVP™ awards, three NBA™ Finals MVP awards, two scoring titles and (14) All-NBA™ team selections. Shaq has also released four rap albums, has starred in numerous films and television shows, and is currently featured in numerous commercials. As of 2019, his net worth is roughly $400 million, with most of his income coming from endorsements and other business ventures. He is the owner of (155) Five Guys Burger ™ joints, (150) car washes, and (17) Auntie Anne's Pretzels™, just to name a few. What is the point? Although Shaq can no longer earn a living on the court, he now lives off his knowledge of basketball and all the residuals that came from him utilizing his talents to the fullest as an NBA™ player.

If you are still questioning whether you have potential left to offer, look at the late Dorothy Steel, who at the age of 92 became a cast member of the third highest-grossing movie of all time, Marvel's *Black Panther*™. As a divorced single mother, she worked most of her career for the Internal Revenue Services and retired as a senior revenue officer assigned to the Virgin Islands. Dorothy's true passion was helping others, so she decided to become a volunteer at a local senior citizen center. Sometime after joining, she signed up to be one of the actresses in a play that the staff was performing for the residents of the senior center. What's amusing is that at the age of 82, Dorothy took on the role of a sassy teenager. At that point in her life, others saw her natural ability. More importantly, in the latter portion of her life, she discovered something about which she was extremely passionate. She eventually attended acting school and landed her first acting role at age 89! Steel also played minor character roles in several high-profile films including *Poms*, *Jumanji: The Next Level*, and her final film, *Black Panther: Wakanda Forever*. Dorothy Steel continued to live out her passion until she died in 2021 at the age of 95.

"If you are still looking for excuses, there are no more left!

THE UNKNOWN POWER WITHIN

There is a well-known story about two young boys who were skating in a frozen pond when suddenly, one of them fell through the ice and got trapped. His friend started to punch the ice in hopes of breaking it, but he was unsuccessful. In desperation, the friend climbed a tree and broke off a huge branch. He came back down the tree and started smashing the ice, eventually breaking it and miraculously saving his friend.

A rescue unit arrived to find that the boy was now safe, but they stood there in amazement, wondering how in the world this little boy could manage to break off a large branch from the tree and smash it through the ice to save his friend. On hearing their conversation, an old man walked up and said, "The boy was able to do it because there was no one here to tell him he couldn't." Too often, we allow our doubts, our fears, circumstances, and the opinions of others to turn us away from tapping into our powerful potential. Although God has equipped us with great potential and the ability to do mighty things, it means nothing if we do nothing with it.

FULL TANK BUT STUCK IN NEUTRAL

Being full of potential and allowing it to remain dormant in your heart is like having a souped-up convertible with tons of horsepower just sitting outside in the driveway. You jump in it and rev it up, and from time to time, you may take it out on a brief test drive around the block, but it never hits the open road. It is always full of gas, but it goes nowhere. The outside appears flawless, and there is no wear on the tires because it never travels far enough to experience the rough roads ahead. In the same way as an unused sports car, many people are full of potential but for whatever reason, are secretly afraid to step on the gas and step out on faith. We allow our fears to paralyze us; therefore, we never take a risk, have trust and faith and go forward with God's tools.

It wasn't until I stepped into my own unused potential did I realize that I had the ability to improve my life and the lives of others so significantly. Up until then, I had the tendency to think lowly of myself and overly esteem others. I was that person with that beautiful car, full of gas and with enormous horsepower, but I was gingerly putting my foot on the pedal, only allowing myself to go so far and then pump on the brakes.

How many times have you been revved up about starting a business, writing a book, or going back to school, but when the time came, you allowed your mind to talk you out of doing what God had placed in your heart? What you think of yourself will ultimately dictate your actions. Thinking small will cause you to coast through life, doing 35 mph in a 75- mph lane in a car built to do 225 mph. While choosing to play it safe and not maximize your potential, you allow self-doubt and low self-esteem to justify why you are stuck in your parking space while watching everyone else pass by.

Ralph Waldo Emerson, an American essayist, and poet, once said, "The only person you are destined to become is the person you decide to be." So, pause for a moment and ask yourself, "Who have I decided to become?" And remember, whenever you place life's obstacles and limitations above your potential, you can only go as far as you think you can.

DON'T LET OTHERS KEEP YOU STUCK

There was a man who saw a line of adult elephants and was amazed that these huge creatures were held by only a small rope tied to their front leg. No chains, no cages. It was apparent that the elephants could at any time break away from the cords they were bound to, but for some reason, they did not. Then the man saw a handler nearby and asked why the gigantic animals just stood there and made no attempt to get away. The controller replied, "When they are young and much smaller, we used the same size rope to tie them, and at that age, it's enough to hold them. As they grow up, they are conditioned to believe they cannot break away. They believe the rope can still hold them, so they never try to break free." These ropes were no match for these huge elephants' potential and brute strength. They clearly possessed the ability to break free at any time from their bondage, but they did not *believe* they could and remained stuck right where they were.

One reason we stay stuck in neutral and do not go any-where is that we focus on the opinions of others and what *they believe* we should be doing. Instead, we should solely focus on what God has proposed for our lives. We are all unique, therefore, a one-size fits all approach is not going to work for everyone. Sometimes we are willing to accept the advice of unqualified people. Dave Ramsey, finan-cial radio show host, and author, once said, "Don't take financial advice from broke people. Find people who have succeeded and do what they do." This not only holds true concerning finances, but also in other areas of life. Seek knowledge from those who actually have it to give. If you accept the opinions of people who are not qualified to give you sound advice, this can be a hindrance to your ability to uncuff your potential.

In the eyes of David's father, brothers, King Saul, and Goliath, David was just a foolish boy with merely a slingshot and a few stones. But in the eyes of God, David was an anointed king with hidden potential. Despite the odds that were against him, he understood that God had already given him a purpose and great potential long before anyone else had that opinion of him. Be like David and know your worth. Know that what you possess was given to you for the betterment of all humanity. Make a commitment today that you will succeed in whatever you put your mind to do.

WHO ARE YOU HANGING WITH?

You may need to get used to the fact that not everyone is going to witness your potential. Sometimes you may make the mistake of trying to get people to see your vision when they have no vision of their own. People who have no concept of their future tend to live in their past, and consequently, they may not be able to see you beyond their knowledge of you. They see you as the same little child whose diaper they use to change or the same kid you were in high school. For this reason, you may find yourself beginning to outgrow some relationships. As time goes on, you begin to discover that your perspectives are not the same as theirs, and what you are passionate about differs. There is a saying, "If you're the smartest person in the room, you're in the wrong room." This means that if you are only around people who *you* are constantly pouring wisdom and knowledge into, but they have nothing to offer to you, chances are they will drain you of your energy. But when you are in the company of someone, and you notice each other's potential, you both glean something from the relationship.

Being in the presence of skilled and like-minded people is essential for personal growth and development. There are certain people that I love talking to because I always gain something enlightening from the conversation. I like talking to those who cause me to take notes and even look up what they're talking about on Google™. On the other hand, it is quite annoying to talk to people who only reiterate things from the past and speak negatively about the present and future. I try to stand clear of people like this and instead surround myself with people that are in places or going in the direction that I would like to be. Oftentimes, a person only goes as far in life as the people they hang around. There came a time when I had to cut ties with friends from my youth because of their willing-ness to remain stagnant. Having an allegiance to people based on the fact that they were a relative, a childhood friend, or even someone who helped me in the past, was not a good enough reason to stay in a relationship that did not help me to grow. This does not mean that I stopped caring or ignored them, but I decided who I would invest my time with going forward. As for you, I suggest you also reassess the people you are hanging with, and if they are not adding any value to your life, then get in the presence of those who will make you feel passionate about your potential.

A few years ago, I listened to a sermon by Bishop T. Jakes. In his message, he was referencing the story when Mary (the mother of Jesus) visited her cousin Elizabeth, who was six months pregnant with her son, John the Baptist. The Bible says that when Elizabeth heard Mary's greeting, the baby leaped in her womb and she became filled with the Holy Spirit. *(Luke 1:41, NIV, Holy Bible).* His point was that if you want to grow, you need to be in the presence of people who can make your *"baby leap."* Someone who is pregnant with purpose and can see that you are as well can wisely assist you in bringing your dreams to full-term.

OTHERS MAY SEE YOUR POTENTIAL

Who you spend your time with is important. You want to be around people who can see your potential even when you cannot. Well-known Gospel music singer-songwriter

Bishop Marvin Sapp, winner of several Singer/Song of the Year Awards, almost did not publish a particular song he wrote. In September of 2006, Sapp's beloved father passed away. Heartbroken by his loss, three days after the funeral, Bishop Sapp was about to close out his church's Sunday service when he thought about his dad and began to sing from his heart. The lyrics simply said, "Never Would Have Made It (without you)."

Around this time, Sapp was working on an album named *"Thirsty."* To his wife Melinda's surprise, he had no intentions of recording the song, "Never Would Have Made It." She convinced him to release the song as the album's first single. What was to him, an impromptu song expressing his love for his father, in 2007, became the No 1 song on the *Billboard* Hot Gospel Songs chart. The song topped the gospel chart for 46 weeks and was also certified platinum *(Unsung, TV One™)*. Even though Bishop Sapp wrote the song, his wife had the vision for it.

We all have potential, some we see very clearly, and some that are seen more clearly by others. In many cases, our potential is apparent to us, but we allow fear and concerns of failure to cause us to hide it. I have seen people with beautiful voices in churches refusing to sing in choirs and high school classmates with great talent turning down opportunities to play for their respective sports teams. It is great to be acknowledged and encouraged by others who see your greatness, but for it to manifest in your life and touch the world, you first have to perceive yourself as being great and be passionate about what you do.

Connecting to people with similar views and values is a key ingredient to your success. Being talented alone is not enough if you do not have the wisdom to use it. This is why I advise you to invest in a coach who can mentor you and see some of the things ahead of you that you might not see. Surround yourself with people who will challenge you to go deeper and tap into the potential that you didn't know existed. You need to get around people that will cause you to feel a little intimidated and inferior, so much so that it lights a flame in you to read and study more. Adopt their attitude and allow their drive and enthusiasm to motivate and encourage you to believe that you, too, have what it takes to be successful. Through their success, inspire yourself to remain disciplined and focused on your vision and goals. Your potential is a gift from God designed specifically for you. It is what sets you apart from others and can bring you great wealth in every area of your life. But it is meaningless if you don't use it.

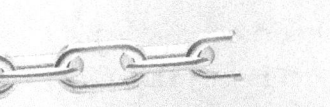

CHAPTER VI

USE YOUR POTENTIAL

There lies within each person a huge reservoir of untapped potential for achievement, success, happiness, health, and greater prosperity.

Jim Rohn

Entrepreneur, Author, and Motivational Speaker

THERE IS MORE IN ME

I once had a co-worker who, at the time, was in his mid-50s, believed that he had no gifts or talents within himself. All he knew to do was work. He worked hours upon hours of overtime only to go and work additional hours at a part-time job. Then one day, seemingly out of nowhere, he woke up and could not move. He was experiencing paralysis in his lower extremities. Flat on his back and looking up at the ceiling, he was in utter shock and fear. For the next five months, he would find himself in a rehabilitation facility trying to do something that we all take for granted; walk again.

As months went on, he promised himself that he would walk out of the rehab center without the aid of a cane or walker. He worked hard to achieve his goal and eventually was able to walk 5 miles a day on the treadmill. This was a great accomplishment, but knowing he could still not perform his duties as a police officer, he emotionally decided that his career was over. With his health being his chief concern, he felt the looming trepidation that he would likely never work again.

Believing all was lost, he came into headquarters one early afternoon to tell the captain his prognosis. With his head down and filled with sadness, he was prepared to call it quits. To his surprise, even with a very pronounced limp, the captain saw potential left in this officer. Because of his long tenure as an officer and his great work ethic, the captain offered him a position he could not refuse. It was a menial position, far less than he was qualified for, but he embraced it with much gratitude and performed his duties to the best of his ability.

Nevertheless, the glorious ending to this story is that this officer never gave up on himself. He decided to triumph over his infirmity and fight, not just for his ability to walk, but also to display to the world what he possesses inside. The job may have been reduced to less than his potential, but what he discovered about himself was immeasurable. It wasn't about the job; it was about finding the courage through major adversity to finish his career and retire on his own terms. At age 56, it was obvious that he was not going to be able to do what he did as a 25-year-old rookie, but what he learned in the process is that he still had potentially left in his tank.

NEVER UNDERESTIMATE YOUR GIFTS

A man's gift opens doors for him and brings him before great men.

Proverbs 18:16

Berean Study Bible

You may be someone who does not believe they have the credentials to do something great in the world. As a result, you may think less of yourself because you draw your self-worth from what society deems acceptable, focusing on the latest trends on social media or even trying to 'keep up with the Kardashians'. Do you ever compare yourself to others who are excelling in life? When you do, doesn't it seem like *everyone* around you is starting their own businesses, driving new cars, buying bigger homes in nicer neighborhoods, or graduating from college? I can assure you that if you are constantly inundating your thoughts with the successful lifestyles of others, you will ultimately make yourself insecure. But know that God does nothing in vain. The fact that He created us and we are still breathing means He has something for us to do.

Regardless of your lack of experience or education, God can use ordinary people to do extraordinary things! Jesus proved this when He began His ministry in the city of Galilee. Jesus went along the sea and began recruiting ordinary fishermen to mentor to become God's world-changers."And Jesus, walking by the Sea of Galilee, saw two brothers, Simon called Peter, and Andrew his brother, casting a net into the sea: for they were fishermen. Then He said to them, 'Follow Me, and I will make you fishers of men." They immediately left their nets and followed Him." —Matthew 4:18-20.

What the world considers ordinary or inadequate does not matter. God sees you to be perfect for His use because He knows what He created you for. So, I encourage people never to put the phrase, "I'm just a(n)" in front of what they do. For example, some will say, "I am just a" security guard, waitress, or usher at my church. Some may perceive these as menial positions, but without these people, the organizations they represent cannot function properly.

In life, we all have a role to play. Some will be more intricate than others, but all are important. A perfect example is an arm. I am sure you will agree that the arm's bicep is the most appealing part. Unlike the elbow, it gets all the notoriety. It gets featured on the covers of fitness magazines and videos. Nevertheless, the elbow is vitally important because the bicep cannot flex and reach its full potential without the presence of the elbow.

However, many view their value to the world based on standards created by the status quo, and as a result, they tend to settle into a daily routine of working for someone else while doing something outside of their passion. By doing so, you are concealing your potential and underutilizing your gifts and talents. Always remember that no matter what profession you desire or skills you possess when God gets involved in it, He can give you the power, wisdom, and know-how to do much more. Whether you do not have the money or the credentials, He can give you just one talent along with His anointing; from it, another can manifest, and then another. You don't have to have numerous talents; all you need is ONE. Remember, Dr. George Washington Carver was able to create more than 300 products from ONE peanut. So, do not bury what you have been given to work with because the possibilities from that one skill are endless.

APPLY IT!

Knowledge is like paint; it does
no good until it is applied.

Doe Zantamata
Author, Artist, and Photographer

Yes, I was guilty as charged. I became an *information junkie* who stored up knowledge from YouTube™ videos, books, audiobooks, webinars, seminars, and whatever correspondence I could find. I could quote Lisa Nichols, Jim Rohn, Les Brown, Melanie (Mel) Robbins, and all of the great speakers and motivators. There was only one problem, I did not use the tools of perspective, passion, or potential. Therefore, I set no goals and was no closer to fulfilling my purpose. All of the nuggets they dropped in my spirit and all of the power quotes I memorized laid dormant in my mind, rendering me ineffective. I allowed fear and concerns of failure to keep me from launching out of my personal wilderness.

IDENTIFY YOUR FEAR, THEN DO IT AFRAID

Courage is not the absence of fear, but
rather the judgment that something else
is more important than fear.

Ambrose Redmoon
Writer and former manager of psychedelic folk rock bands

The word **F.E.A.R** is an acronym for *False Evidence Appearing Real.* In other words, fear is simply an unpleasant emotion that derives from negative beliefs about oneself or circumstances that are not true. For as long as I can remember, I have always been afraid of making mistakes.

My *perspective* of myself hindered me from seeing a successful future. Because I could not see a bright future, whenever I felt *passionate* about something, it never materialized because I never believed it could happen. Even though I knew I had *potential*, I could not get myself to believe I was good enough. This left me feeling as if I did not have a *purpose* for my life, and without a purpose, it was impossible to have a *plan* for my future. Being afraid made me apprehensive about taking chances, and whenever I did step out to take on an endeavor, most times, I never finished what I started. I was self-sabotaging, creating self-imposed limitations.

As I mentioned earlier, working at the nursing home right after graduating high school started off okay, but after a while, concerns about what my future held hovered over me. Being uncertain kept me imprisoned in my own mind and the thought of spending decades locked up in a dead-end job utterly frightened me. I knew that if I didn't do something different, then nothing would change. I had to make a move despite fear and uncertainty. I had to do it afraid and take a chance. At age 24, I took a leap of faith out of my comfort zone, and over a 29-year period, I began and completed a successful career in law enforcement. If I would have allowed fear to keep me in handcuffs, I would have never experienced the awesome career I had as a police officer.

TAKE A CHANCE ON YOURSELF

According to the Census Bureau, more than 4 million new businesses were created in the U. during 2020 — the highest total on record. For reference, that's a 24% increase from 2019 and 51% higher than the 2010-19 average. Half a million new businesses were started in January 2021, alone. Many were probably life-long dreams finally coming to pass, and others were created out of desperation due to the effects of the pandemic. Whatever their motives were, they found strong enough reasons, strength, and determination to do it. Many people saw things from a new *perspective* and decided to go after their *passions*, and realized they had *potential* far beyond the work they were doing for their employers. Maybe they began to imagine themselves living a life of *purpose* that provided them with a *plan,* time, and financial freedom that their job could never offer. Taking a chance on themselves allowed them to uncuff their creative abilities and experience life more on their own terms.

MENTALLY INCARCERATED

Your present circumstances don't determine where you can go, they merely determine where you start.

Nido Qubein,

An American-Jordanian Businessman and Motivational Speaker

Thinking outside the box is not unusual for my cousin, Sharon. She was the youngest of 14 children who were all groomed by their parents to be risk-taking entrepreneurs. I have always admired Sharon for her sweet spirit but also her grit and tenacity. Raised in a Christian home by parents who were well respected in the community, it came as a great surprise when Sharon's life began to spiral out of control. In the early 1990s, Sharon and her sister Becky started cleaning houses in the affluent suburbs of Philadelphia, Pa. They had discovered a market that proved to be quite lucrative as they were creating credibility within the community.

As their unofficial business grew, so did Sharon's secret drug habit. Having full access to their client's homes, Sharon took blank personal checks, endorsed them, and cashed them. Over time, she was eventually caught, prosecuted, and sentenced to six months in prison. Being afraid of Incarceration and unsure of her future, Sharon found herself weeping and praying for support. Suddenly, she was overwhelmed with a sense of peace and heard a message in her spirit that simply said, "I got you." Sharon knew at that moment that this message was from God, giving her a second chance. She discovered that if the Lord forgave her and still had a plan for her, she had to commit to rebuilding her life and stand clear of trouble. Sharon felt good about herself again despite being behind prison walls because she saw a glimpse of who she was and what she was capable of accomplishing. There she wrote out her goals and plans to grow her business.

Fortunately, upon her release, she was drug-free and could continue working with her sister, Becky. Despite her past circumstances, in 1995, Sharon became President and CEO of S&B Organic Cleaning Services—a full-service commercial and residential cleaning service. Sadly, Becky passed away some years later, but Sharon not only maintained the business, by 2018, she was also able to grow it to seven figures. Despite her setback, Sharon continued to believe in herself. She could have believed that she messed up too much to be trusted ever again to work in her field. Nevertheless, she stuck with what she was good at and did not deviate from her plan.

If you are in a similar situation where you are physically incarcerated, or you are mentally locked up in your personal jail cell, I urge you to make a decision that you are going to take a chance on yourself. You must be willing to put your money on yourself to win, even when the odds are against you. Free yourself from the bondage of complacency and fear that keeps you bound from discovering what your purpose is. Unleash your passion right now! Let Sharon's story be a glimmer of hope for you that no matter what twists and turns your life may take, your potential is always inside you and is just waiting to manifest.

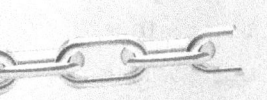

CHAPTER VII

DISCOVER YOUR PURPOSE

*Definiteness of purpose is the starting
point of all achievement.*

W. Clement Stone,

Businessman, Philanthropist, and self-help Book Author

Purpose is defined as "the original intent for the existence of a thing." Purpose answers the age-old questions that frequently escape us; "Who am I? Why am I here? What have I been called to do with my life?" How many times have you ever had that nagging feeling that you were born to do more than what you are doing right now? How many countless days and sleepless nights have you sought to find your reason for existence? For years I struggled with these same questions and emotions. I simply wanted to know my purpose. I was not bothered *that much* by not having enough money, driving a dilapidated car, or not having a college degree. But not being aware of who I was to be in my time on earth left a void in my soul and made me feel as though I was the only person in the universe who didn't know his purpose. Therefore, I had difficulty believing in myself and could never accept the fact that I was good enough.

It can be frustrating to realize that you have a purpose, but you're not exactly sure what it is. And despite your current circumstances and all of your past failures, you find yourself standing on the proverbial *sideline of life*, waiting for someone to call you into the game. Meanwhile, the *clock of life* is quickly winding down, and you're sitting watching every unfulfilled day pass you by. Every promotion or business prospect seems to whiz right past you as you stand there twiddling your thumbs with no inkling of certainty concerning your future. And the loud piercing voices you hear are not coming from the thousands of screaming fans in the stands. The most powerful, compelling voice that you hear is right inside of you! It is your purpose, and it's calling you by name, yelling, "Get in the game! Get in the game!" And, as much as you try to ignore it, you hear it over and over again. Your purpose wants to be discovered by you and help you fulfill your wildest dreams.

WHAT IS MY PURPOSE?

Who am I? And how, I wonder, will this story end?

Nicolas Sparks,

Novelist, Screenwriter, and Philanthropist.

For most people, *who am I?* is probably the most asked question and of great difficulty to answer. No matter your status at this juncture in life, I believe the majority of people struggle to discover their purpose for existing. I believe the struggle to solve these questions derives from the inability to see into one's future. Too often, people lose focus on where they are going because they are so fixated on their past, which hinders them from using their imagination.

What is fascinating to me is that children have no problem answering these questions. If you ask a five- or six-year-old child what they want to become when they grow up, they will not hesitate to answer. Children have such vivid imaginations without any restrictions. They will tell you I want to be a doctor, nurse, football player, chef, ballerina, astronaut, and even a rock star. Children want what they want with no ambiguity, and if they can't get what they want, they will ask, *why not?* Not to be disrespectful, but because they don't see limits. Kids have no concept of can not or lack.

Ironically, when you ask these same questions to youth by age 13, surprisingly, oftentimes the answer is, "I don't know," as they carelessly shrug their shoulders. What happens between the ages of 5 and 13? How does the sureness of the enthusiastic preschooler change so drastically by the time they become a teenager? When they were younger, the things they desired came straight from the heart; they had child-like faith. As they mature, their parents and/or other influential people often challenge their faith by infusing their negative, limiting thoughts into their young. impressionable minds. Instead of continuing to follow their hearts, believing they can have whatever they imagine, they begin to adhere to the constraints that were put in their thoughts. Hence, the understanding of their future and purpose has become uncertain.

YOUR PURPOSE WAS GIVEN TO YOU BY THE MANUFACTURER

Think back to when you were a child and what you wanted to be when you grew up. Remember how often you talked about it with your friends and how you would draw and color it in your scrapbooks. Reflect on the vivid colors on your sports car and the long flowing train on your wedding gown. Has any person or circumstance caused you to abandon your dream and lose sight of your purpose? Those dreams that you had as a child were authentic. They were organic, unadulterated thoughts that were aligned with your life's purpose. No guru could give you those dreams, nor could you get them from a 90-minute webinar. Those vivid seeds of imagination were planted in you by Thee *Manufacturer (God)*. Even if the trials of life have thrown you off course throughout the years, those childhood dreams are still in your heart right where God put them.

YOU WERE CREATED TO SUCCEED

According to the founders of Mercedes-Benz™, their vision was to make the most prestigious luxury car on the planet. As the story goes, Gottlieb Daimler wrote the iconic words *The Best or Nothing* on a piece of paper and placed it in his factory to inspire, provoke, and push his employees to build the best cars in the world. From there, Mercedes put their stamp of approval on every single vehicle created in their manufacturing plant. In 2018, the designers of this iconic entity produced and sold more than 2 million cars. For more than a century, Mercedes Benz™ has stood boldly behind each car they have made. From the A-Class to the S-Class, they have always been the cream of the crop. And because of that mission, the classic Mercedes-Benz™ emblem is revered everywhere for being one of the best. Just as this luxurious line of cars was created with such style, grace, and perfection by its creator, your *Manufacturer* also crafted you with great potential and equipped you with everything you need to be successful. He is proud of who He made you to be and has confidence in your ability to perform. You are capable of doing everything you were designed to do.

YOUR PURPOSE IS THE TICKET TO YOUR DESTINY

No matter where you may find yourself at this stage of your life, whether you are currently unemployed, or a high school dropout, your purpose is still alive within you. You are equipped with the same plan and purpose that was intended for your life. Begin to concentrate on what you do best with the greatest of ease. It may be baking, coaching, designing clothes, or strong leadership and management skills. Whatever it is, do what you must to perfect it, then offer it to the marketplace. When you put your purpose on display to satisfy a need, others will value you and compensate you for what you're worth.

In sports, the gifts and talents of world-class athletes are always on display. Because they are capable of playing at such a high level, people will spend hundreds, even thousands of dollars, to attend an event. At the collegiate level, universities strive to bring in the best talents for their athletic programs. For this reason, college scouts will travel into some of the roughest neighborhoods to recruit top high school athletes. Under normal circumstances, you could not pay college scouts enough money to hang out in the courtyard of a public housing facility and socialize with a 17-year- old black kid. However, they will pay a visit to offer a potential star athlete a full scholarship to their university. Not because they are fond of him or her but for what their athletic prowess would bring to their program. The truth is people are attracted to those with purpose. Those scouts are attracted to those kids with great abilities who are capable of enhancing their mission, which is to win games. They are drawn to those who believe in themselves and that they can accomplish their dreams of making it to the professional level.

People will call upon you because you have what it takes to solve problems. I often express to young people in particular that they were not born to be a problem but to solve them. This is why you cannot afford to continue to waste any more time or your talents because someone is waiting on the gift that God gave you to be a blessing to the world. Whether it is sports, medicine, art, academics, or preaching the Gospel, your *purpose* is the ticket to your success!

DON'T DIE WITH YOUR GIFT!

Pastor Rick Warren once said, "The greatest tragedy in life is not death, but life without purpose." Millions go through life working hard every day. They marry their sweethearts, raise children, and contribute to society, only to die without ever getting in touch with God's very reason for placing them on the earth. I once heard the late-great Dr. Myles Monroe say, "The graveyard is the richest place on the surface of the earth. There, you'll see many unpublished books, ideas that never came to fruition, songs never sung, and dramatic talents never acted upon."

A few years ago, my beloved aunt, Lana, passed away. Although it was a sad occasion for me, I can recall sitting in the sanctuary of the church during her 'home-going' service, beaming with pride as speaker after speaker testified of her significant accomplishments. For decades, she unselfishly touched the lives of so many people by using the wisdom and knowledge God gave her. God shows no partiality. If He gifted my aunt to empower so many, then He has also given gifts to you to fulfill your purpose.

Your purpose is just waiting for you, but it's up to you to discover it. Finding your purpose takes time, and there may be periods of uncertainty as to what is your true calling. For instance, Vera Wang, one of the world's most prominent bridal wear designers, did not initially step right into the field of fashion. Although she grew up in an affluent household on Manhattan's Upper East side, Wang's biggest success didn't happen overnight but came later in life. She experienced a lot of failures and setbacks throughout her journey. Before fashion, she had a great passion for figure skating. She competed professionally as a teenager, but after coming in fifth place in the junior pairs competition at the 1968. Figure Skating Championships™, she decided to give up on her hopes for a spot on the Olympic™ team.[8] In 1971, upon graduation from college, Vera began working for Vogue™ magazine. Within a year, by the age of 23, she was promoted to senior fashion editor and was ultimately elevated to an editorial job, where she stayed for 17 years. At some point, Wang had applied for but lost a bid for the position of editor-in-chief. After failing to make the Olympics team and now losing out on the chief editor's position, she became more motivated and determined to succeed. So, through her connections with Vogue, she went to Ralph Lauren and became a design director for all of his women's clothing divisions.

At age 39, Vera was engaged to be married but had a difficult time finding a wedding gown. Seeing her frustration, her dad saw this as a business opportunity and encouraged her to leave Ralph and start her own company. Although she was hesitant to do so, she followed her father's advice. And with his financial support, after designing her own wedding dress, Wang opened a bridal boutique and soon launched her own signature collection. [9] And today, at age 73, Vera Wang's net worth is $650 million dollars. She

[8] (wwwnbcom)
[9] (wwwoogleom)

has bridal boutiques in London, Tokyo, and Sydney. Her namesake brand has also expanded to ready-to-wear, jewelry, eyewear, shoes, fragrance, and homeware. She has licensing deals with Zales™, Kohl's™, and David's Bridal™ and directly employs more than 200 people. [10]

Ironically, as a designer, Vera Wang first received international attention during the 1992 Olympics Games™ in Albertville, France, when she designed a hand-beaded ensemble for figure skater Nancy Kerrigan. Even though she was not able to follow her passion and participate in the Olympics™, Wang would go on to design outfits for some of the best figure skaters on the planet. Although it took her over two decades to step into her purpose, she never gave up on herself by taking risks that ultimately led to her success.

---

[10] (wwwnbcom)

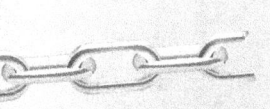

CHAPTER VIII

I KNOW MY PURPOSE

"The greatest discovery in life is self-discovery. Until you find yourself, you will always be someone else. Become yourself."

Myles Munroe

Pastor, Author, Speaker, and Leadership Consultant

A t the time of writing this book, there are approximately 7 billion people worldwide[11]. There is no coincidence or accident that you are here. You were created in the image and likeness of God. That alone should be enough to inspire you to believe that you have the capacity to do great things. You have the DNA of the Creator flowing through you; therefore, you, too, are creative. As a matter

---

[11] *(wwworldometersnfo)*

of fact, there are billions of people around the world who are waiting exclusively for your ingenuity to be unleashed into the universe. The gift that you possess, if used, can enrich someone's life. Ask yourself, what are you holding back from the world? What are you afraid to do that has the potential to change your financial future and be a blessing to your family for generations to come? Ask yourself, where would our world be today concerning technology if it were not for the contributions of people like Bill Gates *(Microsoft™)*, and Robert F. Smith *(Vista Equity Partners™)*, who is currently the wealthiest Black person in the U? How different would our shopping experience be without the innovation of Jeff Bezos *(Amazon™)*, or Pierre Omidyar *(eBay™)?*. Where would we be in the advancement in the medical field without the likes of Maria Siemionow, a Polish transplant surgeon and scientist, or Patricia Era Bath, an ophthalmologist, who invented an improved device for laser cataract surgery? Where would my dream to publish this book be if JB Owen *(Ignite Publishing™)*, who has helped over 700 people publish their personal and transformational stories that span 13 countries, be if she had not pushed past her barriers of being a woman in a male-dominated industry and built a publishing house devoted to empowering authors? Just like them, you have the ability to change the world, but first, you must perceive yourself as the one person out of billions who has the potential to make a powerful impact on humanity.

What idea, invention, belief, dream, or aspiration are you sitting on? What have you been talking yourself out of doing, and why? Whatever you have imagined yourself doing, you *have* to believe it is possible. What you are sitting on *is* the very thing that is associated with your passion and purpose. What you aspire to do *is* in your heart, but you allow fear and doubt to keep you cuffed and bound. You know you're great at it, but the difference between you and others who are flourishing at it is that they stepped out on faith despite being afraid. Do not allow your fears to continue to keep you from presenting your purpose to the world, but instead, unwrap it for all to see, experience, and reap the benefits.

DON'T HIDE WHAT YOU HAVE

"Know what sparks the light in you. Then use that light to illuminate the world."

Oprah Winfrey
American Talk Show Host, Television Producer, Actress, Author, and Philanthropist.

For years, I struggled with self-esteem issues and always had the tendency to look at others with more regard than I gave myself. As a result, I always found myself shrinking back and hiding my light instead of allowing it to shine.

At the age of four, I began playing American football. My brother was five years older than me, and he was my hero, and because he was a huge football fan, I became one also. When I played, I displayed a great talent for such a young child. I was fearless and unafraid of being tackled by the older kids, some being twice my size. I was a rough little guy who was not afraid to get injured or sacrifice my body to make a great play. But somewhere along the way, when I went to high school, although I still played with reckless abandon, still running around like a madman out on the field, unfortunately, as I previously stated, it was difficult for me to see myself going any further. I lacked confidence in myself that I could play at the collegiate level. The talent was there, but instead of displaying it, I hid it and chose to settle for what life would offer me. I let go of my dream of playing professional football and allowed fear to cause me to forsake the thing that I loved all of my life. In my mind, making it to the National Football League (NFL™) could never happen for me.

Throughout adulthood, feelings of incompetence also loomed over me. My light did not shine boldly, strong, and bright as it should have, but instead, it was a constant flickering. I would show signs of greatness, then put it out. My desire for years was to become an inspirational speaker. There were times when I spoke at schools, churches, and other events and received accolades, but I went back into hiding. I would never follow up on opportunities to take my speaking career to another level. Because I opted not to allow my greatness to shine, I became a one-hit wonder instead of reaching my dream of becoming a world-renowned speaker.

After allowing this to go on for years, I became angry with myself, but still not enough for me to take the necessary actions to change. I was letting the fear of messing up or underperforming control my light switch, and as a result, I would talk myself out of going to the next level. I was like an adolescent jumping rope, rocking back and forth, waiting for the perfect time to jump in between the fast-going, double-dutch ropes. But unlike that young person who would eventually jump in, double-mindedness kept me grounded. Consequently, I never jumped into my calling because I was seeking a level of perfection that I would later learn did not exist.

Letting fear rule your life can be rather costly. Not putting it in its proper perspective can cause you to lose out on something that could be a blessing to you and your family for generations to come. Who knows, maybe I could have been drafted into the NFL™ in 1990, along with the great Hall of Fame player, Emmitt Smith, or with Blair Thomas, who was from my hometown. I could have possibly made millions of dollars that could have profoundly changed the trajectory of my life. It took me years later to discover and reconnect with my passion for football, but by then, that window of opportunity had passed me by. Fortunately, I learned from that experience not to ever underestimate myself and hide my gifts. I also learned that gifted, successful people like Beyonce, Pastor Joyce Meyer, Steve Harvey, and others I have admired over the years all admit to being afraid, but they did it anyway. Once I could accept that I can experience fear without allowing it to interfere with my success, I became bolder and more confident. From that point forward, every time an opportunity came, I'd ask myself, "Why not me?" I have a passion for it. I have the potential to do it, and it's in line with my purpose. With this newfound attitude, I was able to accomplish anything I believed I could do.

YOU REAP WHAT YOU SOW

"If you don't like the crop you are reaping, check the seed you are sowing."

- John Maxwell,
An American Author, Speaker, Pastor, and Leadership Expert

Oftentimes when things are not going our way, we tend to look outside ourselves to find the solution to the problem. I know a friend who blames everything and everyone for her issues, never considering her contributions to the matter. If your life is not improving, blaming the weather, the government, a rise in gas, a decrease in pay, and your in-laws will not make your life more productive. Whether you're having relationship issues, weight loss, or financial struggles, you must take ownership that you are a part of the problem and that you hold the key to your solution. An old African proverb says, "If there is no enemy within, the enemy outside can do us no harm." Meaning, if you can learn to overcome the attacks and limitations you put on yourself, then there is not much the world can throw at you that you won't be able to conquer.

How you see yourself is a picture framed in your own head by your own thoughts. It is no different from being a farmer; whatever seed he puts into the dirt, in due time, that is what will come to the surface. Ladies and gentlemen, only you have the power to determine how much you will grow and what you will become. If you want apples, don't plant orange seeds. If you want success, get rid of those seeds of failure, and immerse yourself in an environment where you can cultivate your mind and produce a harvest. No farmer plants corn and comes back and forth to the field with their fingers crossed, praying that tomatoes don't grow.

The Holy Bible tells us that the Children of Israel were promised by God that they would possess a land flowing with milk and honey. The Lord arranged for Moses to send 12 spies to explore the land and come back with a report of what they observed. Only two men out of the 12 spies, Caleb, and Joshua, saw everything God said was available to them. They described seeing clusters of grapes so large that it took two men to carry them along with some pomegranates and figs. The other men gave a different report. Despite being exposed to the promises of God, their primary focus was on the belief that the inhabitants of the land were larger and therefore, stronger than them. In comparison, they saw themselves as grasshoppers and automatically believed that the inhabitants perceived them the same way. As a result of their negative report and their inability to trust God's word, they were not allowed to enter the promised land and ultimately died in the wilderness *(Numbers chapters 13-14, Holy Bible).*

Remember that the words you speak into the atmosphere concerning your life have power that can be of negative or positive consequences. *Life and death are in the power of the tongue (Proverbs 18:21, BSB)* If you are studying diligently and praying for a promotion, then don't follow up your hard work and petitions by telling yourself that you're going to get picked over by your boss for someone more qualified. Your words have power, that's why you must cut off negative thoughts at their roots because once they begin to grow and develop, like weeds, they will choke out any dreams and aspirations you may have.

SEE IT AND GO GET IT!

How many times have you allowed your smallness to talk you out of going after something you desire? There were several times I allowed opportunities to pass me by due to a lack of confidence. Instead of looking at the greatness inside of me, I subconsciously made others bigger and greater than me and hence, saw them living out the promises that I knew were meant for me. Have you ever asked yourself, "Why do I doubt myself? How is it that others can take chances on their abilities with great confidence, and I resist doing so? The truth is simple. It merely comes down to deciding what *you* want. You are either going to do it, or you're not. Others are no different than you, they just decide to do it despite how they feel, whether the timing is right, or if the odds are in their favor. They go after what they want and aim high. They intentionally hit their mark because they only aim at a target that is centered around their purpose. For you to live on purpose, you must first believe that you are capable of doing what you desire. Then once you figure out what you want, sharpen your skills, and go for it.

TAKE A LEAP OF FAITH

A few years ago, comedian, radio, and television personality Steve Harvey wrote a book entitled "Jump." A self-proclaimed college dropout who once lived in his car, Steve became a #1 New York Times™ bestselling author. In his book, he encourages his readers to take a leap of faith to achieve a life of abundance. The Steve Harvey we know today did not start off with wealth and abundance, but once he discovered his gift in comedy, he took a leap of faith, quit his job, and pursued a career in comedy. He says, "Every successful person has jumped. They have taken their hopes and dreams and taken a leap of faith towards them. *If* you desire greatness in your life, eventually, you are going to have to jump."

Taking a leap of faith is never easy. Leaving a place of comfort and familiarity takes courage because you don't know how things will turn out for you. With this in mind, it is up to you to decide whether you want to remain in a place you no longer want to be or take a life-changing jump. Steve says, "The only way to soar is for you to jump. You have to take that gift that is packed away in your backpack, jump off the cliff and pull the cord." He then says, "When you first jump, your parachute will not open right away, but it eventually will. This is a promise from God. It is not a theory-it's a promise." Yes! The gift God gave you is meant to be unpacked and offered to the world. You just have to trust that when you jump, He will be right there with you. This doesn't mean that jumping will not be frightening. You may suffer some bumps and bruises during your journey, and at times it may seem as though your parachute will never open, and hitting rock bottom is inevitable.

Fortunately, the jump Steve Harvey speaks of is only a metaphor that illustrates what steps you must take in order to become successful. In comparison, jumping into your calling is nowhere close to being as frightening or dangerous as jumping from a cliff with a parachute. Looking at taking a leap of faith from this perspective should be more encouraging. Simply trusting in your abilities and putting your all into doing something that you are passionate about may not be as physically costly as having to parachute from thousands of feet in the air. Nevertheless, if you remain grounded, held down by fear, doubt, insecurities, and any other limiting beliefs that you allow to keep you from jumping, that too can cost you from becoming who you desire to be and want for yourself and your family. If you are truly ready to uncuff your potential, then taking a leap of faith is essential.

Seeing others fulfilling their purpose can be intimidating if you are still uncertain of your own. I can attest to the dark feeling of not knowing my true reason for existing and how inadequate it made me feel. That is why I want to ensure that by reading this book, you'll become fully aware of your purpose. I want to know that my ideas help you overcome those fears that are keeping you cuffed and unable to move forward in life. Living on purpose is your true success. Don't consider what others are doing, but instead, focus on what brings your greatest fulfillment. Once you become certain of what gives you that sense of satisfaction, you will have a great insight into your purpose. When you take the time to find your purpose, you open a floodgate of opportunities. You will find yourself attracting people with the same interest as you who can provide the resources you may need. When you step into your purpose, you access the keys to open doors that were locked shut while you were uncertain about your existence.

If you are still uncertain about your purpose, then ask yourself these questions:

1. What did I love to do when I was six years old, and who did I want to become?
2. If I had an abundance of time and money, what would I like to do most?
3. What bothers me enough to take action towards making a difference?
4. If I only had six months to live, what would I do, and how would I want to be remembered?
5. What makes you happy as an adult?
6. What is something that I would regret not doing if I died today?
7. What do I and others believe I do well?
8. How do I influence others?

These questions are important to answer because they give insight into what kind of career or business you would be best suited for. They help you see the path you desire, the beliefs you are holding onto, and the thoughts you have adopted.

I encourage you to take some time out of your day, find a quiet place to collect your thoughts and answer the above questions. Once you have completed that and you have a better idea of who you are, then write down some things that are in your heart to do that you would like to do to make a living (Don't worry about how much money you can make, or whether or not you have ample education; that will come.). When you figure out what you love to do and what is most important in your life, seek out experts to glean from who are already successful in your field of choice and emulate their actions. Find those who have reached your goal and learn from them. Explore how you can develop the skills to become successful in your area of expertise or talent. The world is waiting on you to discover your purpose and once you do, get with those capable of giving you proper guidance to help you create a plan that will empower you to reach your goals. If I can help you, be sure to reach out. I have walked this path and commit to helping those who desire guidance. Things changed for me once I hired a life coach who challenged me to stop resisting the greatness that I possessed. He held me accountable to utilize my gifts and talents and become the person I was capable of becoming. Through my book, coaching, and my online courses, I would love to help you out as well. I want to help *you* create a plan to *unlock your potential!*

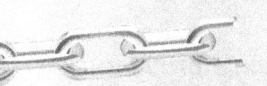

CHAPTER IX

CREATE A PLAN

*Share your plans with the
LORD, and you will succeed.*

Proverbs 16:3

Contemporary English Version (CEV)

*W*hat is planning? Planning is your strategy for success. Without planning for success, none of the previous keys matter. Success occurs not when you discover your purpose but when you fulfill it. If you want to be successful at anything, you must devise a plan. A plan keeps you focused on the goal at hand. It guides you in the direction you want to go. But there will also be times during the planning stages when things will appear not to go as intended. Nevertheless, you must stay the course because if you abort the plan, you will also abort your destiny.

TALK IS CHEAP

Proverbs 14:23 says that *All hard work brings a profit, but mere talk leads to poverty (NIV)*. This is so true. Words without actions are meaningless, and at the end of the day, no one benefits. There came a time in my life when I recognized my talents and realized I had my own unique gifts. I knew they were there, but I only talked about using them. Sometimes I look through old journals or come across scrap papers I had written over the years. I felt shame and disappointment that I had good ideas that never materialized. I read over plans and concepts that remained on the paper, never formulating a plan of action. I was allowing fear, doubt, lack of commitment, and confidence to overrule God's plan for my life. Meanwhile, I sat back and watched others succeed as they acted on their dreams and goals. For years I talked about what I was 'going to do' so much that I had to add an eighth day to my calendar. I named that day "Some-day." "Someday I am gonna do this, or Someday I am gonna do that." I let my fears keep me from forming a plan and taking deliberate action. It was not until I began to live with *passion*, hone my *perspective*, discover my *potential*, recognize my *purpose* and develop a *plan* did I see the greatest version of me.

SUCCESS DOESN'T JUST HAPPEN, IT'S PLANNED

I am sure most of you have heard the saying, "If you fail to plan, you plan to fail." I am positive that one would be hard-pressed to find any successful person who would tell you that he or she became successful by accident. I once heard Oprah Winfrey say that nothing about her life was lucky, but the fact that she was prepared *(for success)* is what set her up to meet opportunities. Today, Oprah is one of the most successful and powerful people in the world. Her rags-to-riches story include growing up living in disfunction with different family members, to being sexually abused by various adult men in her family. Sadly, she became pregnant at the age of 14 by one of her uncles, and her baby boy, who was born prematurely, died in the hospital. Oprah did not have a favorable start, but she always had a plan to become great.

As a child, Winfrey entertained herself by 'play-acting' in front of an 'audience' of farm animals. By age 12, she began making speeches at social gatherings and churches, and one time earned five hundred dollars for a speech. She knew then that she wanted to be "paid to talk." Knowing her passion at such a young age, Oprah attended Tennessee State University after graduating high school and majored in Speech Communications and Performing Arts. At age 19, she became a news anchor in Nashville, TN, for the local

Columbia Broadcasting System (CBS™) television station, then following her graduation from Tennessee State University in 1976, she was made a reporter and co-anchor for the ABC™ news affiliate in Baltimore, MD. A year later, she followed her true passion again and became co-host of the Baltimore morning show *People Are Talking.* Then in 1984, Oprah was hired to help resurrect a morning talk show in Chicago, IL. as an anchor on *A. Chicago. Prior to her arrival, the* ratings for the show were consistently last. Within three months as the anchor, the talk show slightly inched ahead of *The Phil Donahue Show.* Then in September 1985, the program was renamed the *Oprah Winfrey Show,* and in 1986 became syndicated nationally. The program became the highest-rated television talk show in the United States and earned several Emmy Awards.

Oprah would go on to form her own television production company, Harpo Productions, Inc™., and a film production company, Harpo Films™. She also successfully launched O, *The Oprah Magazine™*, Oprah Winfrey Network™ (OWN), and opened a $40 million school for disadvantaged girls in South Africa. She also started in several movies and received numerous awards for her acting and humanitarian work. Despite her rough beginning, Oprah did not allow her circumstances to derail her future plans. She persevered through her problems and never lost sight of her goals. Her philosophy is, "Not only are you responsible for your life but doing the best at this moment puts you in the best place for the next moment." Yes, regardless of what happens to us, we alone are responsible for our outcomes. Just know that every single thing that has ever happened in your life is preparing you for the next moment that is to come. But to be successful, you must devise a plan and stick to it.

CREATE AND FOLLOW YOUR OWN PLAN

The late speaker and entrepreneur Jim Rohn once said: "If you do not design your own life's plan, chances are you will fall into someone else's plan." Just like Oprah, you must create a plan for your life that is centered around your passion and purpose. It is much harder to plan to do something you do not like or around something you're not comfortable doing. Things that I dread doing, I tend to stress about and wait until the last possible minute to do them, and most likely will perform them less efficiently. But the things that I am passionate about that are aligned with my purpose, I am more confident, lively, and energetic when I do them. Unfortunately, because of a lack of planning for one's future, many people are living unhappy and unfulfilled lives that are dictated by someone else's plan. Decide to create your own plan and follow it. Be in charge of your future and use a plan to get there.

GET YOUR PRIORITIES IN ORDER

"The key is not to prioritize what's on your schedule, but to schedule your priorities."

Stephen Covey

Educator, Author, Businessman, and Keynote Speaker

Successful people often give credit to their daily routine as being a great part of their overall success. John Maxwell, who is internationally recognized as being the best in leadership training says, "You will never change your life until you change something you do daily. The secret of your success is found in your daily routine." Planning your day in advance is paramount to your daily success. Every new day can have its own challenges and deadlines to be met, so waking up in the morning without direction can create an unorganized and unproductive day. A great practice for prioritizing your day for greater productivity is writing out your schedule the night before. This allows you to put chores that were not completed onto the next day's list and other assignments that may come to mind. Also, while you are asleep, your to-do list plays throughout your subconscious mind, as it is free from the interference of daily life and external stimuli. While at rest, it has nearly all your brain resources at its disposal. Therefore, make organizing your day a priority. Remember your list of things you are most passionate about from chapter 4 as you prioritize your day. Make sure to incorporate into your plan for the day something that you *like to do,* and not just things you *have to do.* Make this a daily habit.

SUCCESS IS HABITUAL

Successful people are simply those with successful habits.

Brian Tracy,

Canadian-American motivational public speaker and self-development author

James Clear, author of the book *Atomic Habits,* defined habits as "A routine or behavior performed regularly." Habits are formed by us all, some good and some bad. Clear likened them to compound interest for self-improvement, just as money multiplies through compound interest. Also, the effects of your habits multiply as you repeat them. Good and bad habits may not initially seem to make much of a difference, but over a period of time, the impact they deliver can be enormous.

While watching the blockbuster movie King Richard, which portrayed the lives of the two world-renown tennis phenoms, Venus and Serena Williams, I received a more in-depth look into how they became such a dominant force in their profession. Their father, Richard Williams, wanted his daughters to play tennis and decided he would coach them along with his wife, Oracene. He did not only want them to play tennis, but his dream was for them to become world-class champions. He was so serious that he wrote a 78-page plan for the sisters and started training them at the age of 4. The girls were even seen holding tennis rackets in their hands while they were babies in strollers! Although he had very limited resources, Richard was fully committed to making his successful vision for his daughters come true.

Richard introduced the importance of forming good habits to his daughters at an early age. His comprehensive success plan for his future tennis stars included long, vigorous practices. The young sisters hardly ever left the courts, grinding through practice sessions that started as early as 6 a. and stretched into the dark of night after school was out. Some of Richard's neighbors became concerned that he was working the girls too severely and called the police on him for child abuse. When the police arrived at his home, Richard explained to them that he was hard on his girls because he didn't want them to be swept into a culture of drugs and bad people.

Whether or not his methods of teaching his daughters the game of tennis were too harsh, the discipline and structure he brought to their lives created champions. Both girls became professional tennis players by age 14 and throughout their careers, have both been rated No in women's tennis. Venus won seven Grand Slam™ singles titles, five at Wimbledon and two at the US Open. Serena has been ranked No. 1 in the world in singles matches by the Women's Tennis Association™ (WTA) for 319 weeks and finished as the year-end's No. 1 five times. She has amassed 23 grand slam titles in all and has been coined by many of her peers around the world of sports as the Greatest of All Time (G.) in women's tennis. Combined, they have won 122 singles titles, including 30 Grand Slam singles titles, and earned over $175 million in prize money. And while they're considered rivals on the court, they're actually very close — together, they've won 22 doubles titles as teammates, 14 of which have been in Grand Slam™ competitions.

The Williams sisters have dominated the tennis world for decades. Their supremacy on the court did not come by chance, but by the sheer dedication of their parents, who molded them into champions through hard work, discipline, and habits they were taught during their childhoods. Great habits breeds great success, and those habits prepared Venus and Serena for stardom. Without them, they probably wouldn't have ever played tennis at all.

Breaking bad habits and replacing them with good habits is

essential for success. But for most people, this is not an easy task. To help you with this challenge, here are five helpful strategies by James Clear on how to build new habits.

1. ***Start with an incredibly small habit.*** Solve this problem by picking a new habit that is easy enough that you don't need motivation to do it. For example, rather than starting with 50 pushups per day, start with 5 pushups per day. Make it easy enough that you can get it done without motivation.

2. ***Increase your habit in very small ways.*** One percent improvements add up surprisingly fast. So do one percent declines. Rather than trying to do something amazing from the beginning, start small and gradually improve. Along the way, your willpower and motivation will increase, which will make it easier to stick to your habit for good.

3. ***As you build up, break habits into chunks.*** If you continue adding one percent each day, then you'll find yourself increasing very quickly within two or three months. It is important to keep each habit reasonable, so that you can maintain momentum and make the behavior as easy as possible to accomplish. Instead of trying to do 50 pushups at once, breaking it up into 5 sets of 10 might be much easier as you make your way there.

4. ***When you slip, get back on track quickly.*** Top performers make mistakes, commit errors, and get off

track just like everyone else. The difference is that they get back *on track* as quickly as possible. Rather than trying to be perfect, abandon your all-or-nothing mentality. Take some time to consider what will prevent your habit from happening, and how you can plan to work around these issues.

5. ***Be patient. Stick to a pace you can sustain.*** You can make incredible progress if you are *consistent and patient.* If you are adding weight in the gym, you should probably go slower than you think. If you are adding daily sales calls to your business strategy, you should probably start with fewer than you expect to handle. Patience is everything. Do things you can sustain. For more on developing good habits, check out James Clears free download on *30 Days to Better Habits.* (https://jamesclearom/30-days)

IT IS POSSIBLE TO SUCCEED
AT THE WRONG THING

As we just learned the importance of forming good habits, it is also important to develop habits that are centered around your purpose, passion, and potential. Once you have determined what your purpose is and what you are passionate about, then you must establish a sharp focus in the area in which you strongly believe you have the most potential. For instance, some people find themselves deeply passionate about the welfare of young, single mothers who are physically and emotionally abused. This passion may derive from a personal experience or someone they know who was once in that same predicament. Therefore, the strong desire to change the lives of those young women, coupled with the longing to help and influence other people, is where all energy and resources could be directed.

I can recall a time when I was about 19 years old when Mrs. Peggy Mitchell, who is like a second mother to me, referred to me as being a "jack-of-all-trades" (someone who has knowledge of different things but has not mastered any of them). She made this statement to me after I told her I was attending the community college shortly after receiving a trade school certificate where I learned building renovations. She was puzzled, wondering what happened to the trade school degree and why it was necessary to go to another school for something totally different. It was a little embarrassing at the time because I was totally clueless and had no definitive answer or direction for my life. I felt exposed to the world as if everyone but me had a purpose and a plan for their lives. This was an empathetic, pitiful feeling that I would not wish on anyone. Her question chipped away at my self-esteem for many years but eventually taught me that I *must* create a plan for my life and become certain about what I wanted.

MAJORITY RULES

In addition to being undecided in my quest for direction, I also suffered from shyness and lacked self-confidence. I was afraid to take chances, and whenever I did step out to take on an endeavor, most times, I never finished what I started. I was self-sabotaging, creating self-imposed limitations. At that point, I felt lost. Looking back on the situation, I was aimlessly attempting to find my purpose while hiding behind academics to make myself look busy. I was tirelessly working during the day and going to school at night.

Young, innocent, and gullible, I unknowingly subscribed to the same logic as the majority, as others sacrificing their dreams. I was officially caught in the proverbial *rat race* and was trying to fit into a cookie- cutter system that did not cater to my skills and talents. I began to wonder—if the majority rules, then why do only a fraction of people acquire wealth? How is it that decade after decade, the majority go to school, get degrees; work 20, 30, 40, and even 50 years for someone else, and still not be educated enough to succeed?

SPECIALIZED EDUCATION

Later in life, I learned that being specific about what I

wanted for my future was an essential ingredient for my success. Just like a skilled marksman who steadily aims his arrow and hits the target, in the same way, wherever you mostly put your focus is where you will end up. That was my greatest challenge, keeping my mind on one thing long enough to a point of mastery. But I often found myself all over the place. The 19th-century American humorist Josh Billings said it best, "Be like a postage stamp. Stick to one thing until it gets there." In other words, stay with that one thing that you are strongly passionate about and most gifted in, until it delivers.

It is also important to inundate yourself with knowledge by reading books, viewing videos, and attending seminars on topics that are specific to your craft. As you commute back and forth to work, instead of listening to the same songs on the radio, let it be a time of learning. Turn your car into a mobile study. Utilize your time in traffic to tune into the vast numbers of successful people who have achieved the very thing you desire. You can find thousands of tutorials on YouTube™ and gain insight from podcasts and audio books. Remember, success leaves clues, meaning that the people who have accomplished your dreams share their success, giving you step-by-step insight. And, most of the time it is FREE!

Getting a degree is an accomplishment, and indeed, it is a necessity for most upper-level jobs. I suggest if you go to college, seek to obtain a degree in a field that is congruent with your purpose. According to *the National Center for Education Statistics, about 80% of students in the United States end up changing their major at least once, and on average, at least three times over the course of their college career.* That is a considerable percentage of people arbitrarily throwing around thousands of dollars for the sake of "going to college" with no real understanding of why they are there. They follow this well-defined trajectory or go because they were 'told' to go, not fully examining their reasons, intentions, and purpose.

FIND YOUR INSTRUCTIONS

Too often, many people go to school hoping to *find* their purpose instead of using the school as a means to *refine* it. It's like buying white shoe polish before purchasing the shoes, only later to discover that all along you had a desire for black shoes. The point of the story is polish is meant to enhance the shoes, just as education is meant to support your purpose. Many people go to school hoping they will find their purpose there. The great news is your purpose is already inside of you, exactly where God put it. The plan of God for your life is also there. As I mentioned in Chapter 7, *Thee Manufacturer* (God) created you with great potential and equipped you with everything you need to be successful. Everything that was created by man was first planned in the mind. God also had a preexisting plan for your life before he created you. Somewhere inside of you is His stamp of approval, a trademark far more superior than that of Mercedes Benz™, Apple™, Nike™, or any other man-made product. These products made by human hands are amongst the best in their industries, but *you* were made by God. Therefore, you are the Lord's greatest invention. Just seek Him to find the plans He specifically assigned to you and set goals in plans to achieve them.

GOALS, THE ROADMAP
TO YOUR SUCCESS

Most likely, you will not find a successful person who obtained success without a plan, nor will you encounter one who did not have distinct goals established for their life. It is often said, *If you claim to have goals, but they are not written down, then they're just dreams.* Just as an architect looks over the in-depth blueprints of a high-rise building before laying the foundation, you, too, must continually examine your written goals so you can have an unambiguous vision of what you want and what direction you need to go.

I was one who would create goals in my head and never write them down. Psychologist Fitzhugh Dodson once said: "Without goals and plans to reach them, you are like a ship that has set sail without a destination." That was definitely me, but now I can honestly say that writing out my goals is powerful! Viewing my goals daily is a constant reminder of what I said I would do by a specific date and time. When writing this book, I did not begin to show consistent progress until I started setting goals to complete each chapter by a specific time. And every time I finished a chapter, I became even more motivated to meet the next deadline. I saw how powerful having a plan was and learned by creating successful habits that I could indeed reach my goal. I recognized that although it took hard work, it also took belief and faith; in myself! I encourage you to have that same belief and faith in YOU because you'll achieve your goal when you do.

Writing out your goals and completing them one by one is a huge self-motivator. Whether big or small, short or long-term, each time a goal is checked off, it can give you a sense of accomplishment and a desire to produce even more goals for your life. These notable achievements are referred to as *small victories*. Just as exercising good habits consistently has a compounding, positive effect in regard to self-improvement, a series of small victories *(wins)* can also be profoundly rewarding. In his book, *The Power of Habits*, Charles Duhigg uses the term "small wins" to refer to modest behavior changes that can create a chain reaction of more and better changes. *Psychology Today*™ blogger Christopher Bergland also says that "Every small win gives you a spritz of dopamine, that feel-good brain chemical that is linked with motivation" He continues to say that "A series of small wins guarantees a constant supply of dopamine, which is released during goal-oriented behavior and upon achieving a goal.

Setting goals alone is not what is most important to your success, but *completing* them is. Not completing your goals and not keeping your word to yourself can lead to self-doubt and discouragement. Over time, you may even stop believing in your ability to follow through on your promises. If that becomes the case, your goals will never come to fruition. Therefore, let fulfilling your goals be your standard for your life so that you may become accustomed to finishing what you started and keeping your word to yourself. Make completing your goals a top priority, and watch your self-confidence begin to grow as you develop into the person you desire to be.

YOU MUST BELIEVE IN YOURSELF

One of the major roadblocks in the planning phase of my life was my inability to believe in myself. Just as clear as a bright sunny day, you can discover your purpose, you can identify your passion, and the entire world can see your potential. If your perspective of yourself does not change to where *you* see yourself being successful, then your goals and plans are in vain.

My problem was that I could see everyone else fearlessly fulfilling their dreams, while I allowed fear to blind and rob me from doing the same for myself. For too long, I watched others around me give birth to their dreams while I settled again and again with being the proverbial midwife, helping someone else deliver their baby. And another year goes by of me standing with my forehead pressed against the delivery room window, watching and celebrating someone else's creation.

REEVALUATE YOURSELF

At some point, you must be brutally honest and ask yourself the questions, *Why am I not going after my own dreams? In what area of my life do I need to improve? What am I willing to put my all into?* To achieve success, you must first be willing to reevaluate where you are in life and determine if you are doing enough to get to where you need to be. And, if you are not where you want to be, then you must take full responsibility for your whereabouts. You are the sum total of the decisions you have made up to this point, and whatever decisions you make in the future will also determine your outcomes. If you want better outcomes, then stop doing what's not working; pause for a moment, and establish a plan centered around your goals. If you do this you will be part of the committed few who actualize their future. *A Harvard Business Study found that the 3%*

of graduates from their MBA who had their goals written down, ended up earning ten times as much as the other 97% put together, just ten years after graduation. This is encouraging, and reassuring that it is not too late for you to restructure your life.

In addition to reevaluating yourself, you must also reassess your relationships with others and consider how you are spending your time. Obligations to friends and family members can cause you to derail your plans. Although they may want the best for you, they may not understand the time and commitment necessary to achieve your goals. I am not suggesting that you totally cut-out your loved ones, but establish a set time within your plan that will allow you to have a balanced lifestyle consisting of work and pleasure. For example, in addition to working throughout the week, I set aside leisure time for myself on Thursdays, and have date night with my wife every Friday evening. On Sundays, I go to church and relax the rest of the day. No plan will ever be perfect, but in order to achieve the lifestyle you want, put your plans first and try your best not to deviate from them.

Having a clearly defined plan, with clearly defined goals will be the catalyst to get you on your way to success. It is the written recipe to a gourmet meal, the manuscript of an award-winning film, the navigation system that puts you on the right road to your destination. Simply talking about your desires or even writing them down in your journal is not enough to get you to the life you want. You must also create a plan and take action steps toward your goals. Remember, your goals should be centered around your passion, purpose, and what you believe your greatest potential is. Do not let someone else plan your future around what they perceive for you, nor forego your dreams to meet the expectation of the masses. Bear in mind that it is the few, not the majority who are clear and specific about their goals, and are most successful. Therefore, prioritize your days to ensure that you are consistently going in the direction of your goals. Keep believing in yourself, even when others won't, and don't be afraid to work the plan that will ultimately lead you to your destiny.

CHAPTER X

WORK YOUR PLAN

Plan your work and work your plan.
Decide in advance exactly how you
are going to get from where you are to
where you want to go.

Brian Tracy,

a Canadian-American motivational Public
Speaker and self-development Author

There is nothing more satisfying than getting to a place in your life where you planned and achieved it. There is a joyous feeling when all of your dreams, goals, and plans to reach them are all harmoniously composed together like one great symphony. When you think of success stories, we often imagine someone starting off with advantages such as college education and financial support. People who are privileged to attend the best universities and inherit wealth and business ownership. On the contrary, *nearly 68% of the world's richest people are 'self-made,' and only 8% of global high-net-worth individuals were categorized as having completely inherited their wealth.* As I mentioned in the previous chapter, successful people write out their goals, create a plan to carry them out and stick to them. Their success does not come because they were given advantages, instead, they became successful because they created advantages *for themselves* by working on their own plan. That means that the opportunity to become successful is in your favor. Not starting off with various college degrees or a large bank account should not hinder you from achieving your goals. The truth is that once you discover your purpose and create goals and a plan that focuses on what you do best, there is no reason why you can not accomplish whatever you want.

PLAN AROUND YOUR PASSION

A very dear friend to my wife and I is Sharmarro Leak, who is the founder and CEO of Sallicious Catering™. Sharmarro and I first met at our church and served together in the culinary ministry. She was an amazing cook who had a passion to serve others. It was quite obvious that her service was beyond being a volunteer, it was her calling. When Sharmarro was a young girl, she grew up watching her mother and grandmother prepare all types of meals, from daily family dinners to large meals like Thanksgiving and Christmas. Oftentimes, she would help by preparing takeout platters for customers from the community that came by to buy dinners being sold by her family. By the age of 16, Sharmarro was promoted from preparing platters to cooking food. Back then, it seemed more like punishment to her, having to cook in a hot kitchen while all of her siblings and friends were outside having fun. Out of frustration, she even asked her mom and grandma, "It's five of us (her and four siblings), why me? Why do I have to always do the cooking?" She would discover later in life that what appeared to be a burden was actually a blessing.

STICK TO YOUR PLAN AND FULFILL YOUR PURPOSE

Years later, having a family of her own to cook for, Sharmarro's passion for cooking and serving has grown deeper. Although she has a good job in human services, she knew she was not fulfilling her potential. By this time, her grandmother had passed away; sadly, in 2007, her dear mother Sally had passed on too. Though devastated by her loss, she decided to take action and focus her energies on keeping the legacies of her mother and grandmother alive through their recipes. In 2008, Sharmarro Leak unveiled "Sallicious Catering™" to the world. The name is derived from cleverly combining her mother's name, Sally, with the word 'delicious' together.

For the first few years, Sallicious Catering™ was no more than a side hustle at best, taking on small to medium events here and there. At times, it was very taxing physically, emotionally, and financially. Then after seven years of working at her business, things became even worse when her husband had a tragic motorcycle accident in which he severely damaged his leg. As a result, the family's income was now reduced to one. While naturally upset, Sharmarro began to pray for her husband and her business when she heard down in her spirit, "Everything you need to be financially secure is already inside of you." She knew then that she had to stay the course because failure was not an option.

Today, Sallicious Catering is vastly growing in Philadelphia, Pa., and the surrounding states. Sharmarro has become a social media sensation as she does a weekly live cooking show with her aunt called *Cooking with Aunt Sha-Sha*. She was also featured on a local television station for feeding hospital staff and school children in her neighborhood. This philanthropic trait came from her mother, Sally, who did the same when Sharmarro was a child. She also learned from her mother that when times get tough, trust God and continue to work the plan He gave you.

LEARN FROM YOUR MISTAKES

"The only real mistake is the one from which we learn nothing"

Henry Ford,

an American Industrialist, founder of the Ford Motor Company™

Creating a plan for your life is important because it allows you to map out where you are going. Yet in reality, despite our due diligence, plans will not always be successful. Somewhere along the way, mistakes will happen. If you don't believe me, just keep living and you are bound to experience a few. I have made many mistakes and some that I truly regret. Some cost me more than others, but over the years I've learned that there is a lesson in every error. As damaging as mistakes can be, whether it is in relationships, business, or personal endeavors, you cannot afford to miss the lessons or the blessings they have to offer you. No one wants to make a mistake, but doing nothing is even worse. If you do nothing, you learn nothing. Mistakes can be evaluated and corrected, allowing you to adjust your original plan into an even greater plan. Having no plan of action eliminates the possibility of making mistakes that can give you insight into what to do next. Think back to a mistake in your past that became a blessing, and if you dig a little deeper, you may find that there was a great deal of wisdom and even a silver lining that came from it.

Two-time NFL Super Bowl™ winner and Hall of Fame inductee, John Elway was not just one of the greatest quarterbacks in the history of the game, but he was also ranked the 23rd greatest 100 player of all-time. Although he was the first overall player to be selected by the Denver Broncos™ in the 1983 NFL™ Draft, and was already being compared to some of the greatest quarterbacks, Elway had a subpar rookie season. At times he performed so poorly that he was benched by his coach and was severely booed by the Denver fans. He eventually matured into the high-level player he was expected to become and would eventually lead his team to three super bowls. Unfortunately, they lost all three and the talk around the league questioned Elway's ability to win the *big game (the Super Bowl™)*.

In addition to off-season training and sharpening his skills, the best thing he did for himself was develop a *short memory*. This is a mindset that many athletes adopt when it comes to making mistakes. So, when Elway makes a bad play, he instantly puts it in the past and goes on to the next play. The same goes for life. As I previously said, we all will make mistakes, but to progress through them you must be able to put them in your distant memory. Now it is up to you how you relate to that memory. You can either be haunted by it, or you can learn from it. As the late Japanese martial artist, Morihei Ueshiba once said, "Failure is the key to success; each mistake teaches us something."

Before ending his iconic career, John Elway would go on to guide his team to two consecutive Super Bowl™ victories. Because he was thrust into the starting line-up as an inexperienced rookie, and played against tough, experienced opponents, his weaknesses were exposed and he was able to make adjustments. Today, he is in the NFL™ Hall of Fame and is near the top of every statistical category for quarterbacks. Currently, Elway is a successful top executive for the Denver Broncos™ organization. He took his mistakes and learned from them. They became his life lessons, and from them, he developed wisdom and a greater understanding of how to play the game. Despite his tough start, a successful career still awaited him.

YOUR DESTINY AWAITS YOU!

"You nourish your soul by fulfilling your destiny."

Howard S. Kushner,

Rabbi and Author

A few years ago, on a frigid winter morning, I was leaving my home in Philadelphia, PA, to fly to my cousin's house in sunny San Diego, CA. As I walked out of my front door bundled up in my big winter coat, I was met by a burst of crisp, cold air that felt like standing in a walk-in freezer. Upon stepping onto my top landing, I realized that my stairs were covered in a sheet of ice. Icicles were hanging from my railing and overhead awning. To safely get from my house to my car, I had to break the layer of ice off of my steps and sidewalk. I rubbed my cold hands together as I gingerly drove to the airport due to all the icy patches on the road. That caused traffic to travel at a much slower pace than normal. It took me ten extra minutes to arrive, but I eventually made it.

I had taken the first step despite the cold conditions to get to my end destination, which would be a much-needed vacation. Despite starting the day in sub-freezing temperatures and obstacles, I never lost sight of my destination, getting to warmer weather. I had a plan and knew exactly where I was going and how I would get there. Regardless of the icy conditions, I was prepared for my journey, and my plan kept me focused and moving forward. Although I started my day in a cold place, my suitcase was packed with warm weather clothing for where I was going. In just a few hours, my flight landed in sunny San Diego, where it was a very comfortable 78 degrees. That afternoon, my cousin and I were hanging out enjoying the warm Southern California weather. I was wearing short pants and a short-sleeved shirt, completely the opposite of what I was wearing in the morning.

The moral of the story is, starting off in a cold, unfavorable place doesn't mean you must remain there. You have the potential to reach your desired goal, but you must be willing to change your mindset and shift your environment to get there. It does not matter where you start off, your destiny still awaits you! Currently, you may find yourself in a cold place: that place may be a dead-end job, swimming in a pool of debt, going through a divorce, or trapped in a mindset that feels like a maximum-security prison. Nevertheless, your destination is on the other side of your dilemma, but you must take action to reach it. You have to have a desire to leave where you *are* and prepare for where you are *going*. To get out of Philadelphia on that frigid winter morning, and arrive in warm San Diego, first I had to save the funds, coordinate the travel, book the flight, and then show up at the airport. Too often, people get the desire to do something like travel the world but never take the steps or plan out what is needed to make it unfold. They view the resort's website, price the plane tickets, and buy the luggage, but they allow circumstances to keep them from following through. No matter how much you want to see Niagara Falls, the Eiffel Tower, or the Serengeti, it will never occur if you are unwilling to take the necessary steps to get there. Not taking action keeps you cuffed and bound in exactly where you are. Free yourself and enjoy all you dream of by mapping out how to get there and then moving with purpose in that direction.

TAKE ACTION

"Take action! An inch of movement will bring you closer to your goals than a mile of intention."

Steve Maraboli,

A Behavioral Scientist, Speaker, and Author

Getting to where you want to go requires action. It's quite simple; you will either get there , or you won't. The action does not discriminate, but it responds to whoever takes it. To the farmer that took the action of sowing reaped a harvest in its due season. The gymnast who put in countless hours of practice received an Olympic™ gold medal as her reward. Simply filling out the admissions application doesn't equate to a master's degree, but it is the act of studying. Getting from where you are to where you want to be requires *action*. Whether you are driving a $90,000 Range Rover™, or a $9,000 Toyota™, it will not get you to your destination if you do not start the ignition and put the gear in drive. The soft leather, climate-controlled seats, nor panoramic sunroof will not matter if the owner doesn't get the car into motion.

Action is the culmination of your perspectives, passion, potential, purpose, and plans. Taking action will enable you to uncuff your potential and release yourself from the bondage you currently find yourself in. Your goals will *never* happen if you fail to take action. Action is the difference between you becoming that business owner, getting down to your dream weight, receiving that promotion, living debt free, or whatever you desire to have. You will not go forward without working through the plan you created for yourself. There comes a time when you have to stop planning to do something and simply TAKE ACTION! Success is never achieved by just talking about it.

ACTION STEPS

You don't have to see the whole staircase, just take the first step.

Rev. Dr. Martin Luther King Jr.,
Pastor and prominent Civil Rights Leader

In life you will never see the full picture that is going to lead you to your accomplishments, but know that everything you need to succeed in life is already inside of you, *batteries included!* You are God's greatest creation, skillfully crafted and wired for success! And, when you begin to use the 5 keys I have shared, *Purpose, Passion, Potential, Perspective,* and *Planning* you will unlock your potential and unveil your true magnificence! You will have the tools you need to live the amazing life you desire!

Action means taking constant action consistently; not doing one thing, one time. You have to adhere to taking action over and over again. If you don't take action, it is impossible to winhe amazing, four-time Champion and Hall of Fame inductee of the National Hockey League (NHL), Wayne Gretzky, once said, "You miss 100% of the shots you don't take." This means that if you fear taking a chance on yourself because you do not believe that fulfilling your dreams is possible because you do not have enough money, skills, or education, then you will never succeed. Don't let yourself or anyone else talk you out of taking the necessary action you need to take to reach your destiny. Every successful person had to take that first step, a leap of faith, to get to where they are today. Once you do so as well, only then will you, in fact, reach your goals.

Below is a list of things you can do daily that will bring you closer to what you desire and form habits that will help you to become more focused and build up your confidence.

Perspective: Expand your vision by reading something inspiring every day.

Passion: Discover those things you have always wanted to do and just do them.

Potential: It is not what you have used up but what you have left to give. Dig deep.

Purpose: Ask yourself: Who am I? Why am I here? What have I been called to do with my life? Once you know those answers, go out and live your life to the fullest.

Planning: If you want to be successful at anything, you must devise a plan to stay focused on your goals... Yes... You have to stay focused!

Committing to these steps will help you identify who you are and help you to get on course to your desired outcome. Believe in yourself and take a shot at your goals. Wayne Gretzky, considered by many to be the greatest player in the history of the National Hockey League (NHL™) said, "You miss 100% of the shots you *don't* take." This quote is coming from a 4-time champion who scored the most goals in the NHL's history, but he also admits that he probably *missed* more shots than any other player in the league. There is no guarantee you'll make every shot you take, you may only hit 1 out of 100. But that one shot you do take, may be the one that will change your life. It may be the one that allows you to retire early, travel the world, put your children through college, start your own business, or build your dream home. Committing to these steps is committing to yourself and your future. Taking the necessary steps to achieve your dreams may be difficult but, without a doubt, worth it!

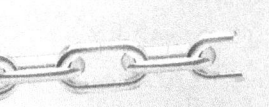

CHAPTER XI

START RIGHT WHERE YOU ARE

"The hardest step is taking the 'first' step."

Lady JB Owen,

Author, Speaker, Publisher, and Knighted Dame.

Now that you have learned the five fundamental ways to uncuff your potential and create your greatest life, the rest is up to you. What you do when you close this book, is what will make a difference in your life. It is true the hardest step *is* taking the 'first' step. But today, I inspire you to simply *start right where you are.* I encourage you to read this book over and over again, go through each principle one by one, and extract the main points that pertain to you, then apply them to your life. You already know what resonates in your spirit and how it motivates you to *want* to take action. You know the areas in your life where you feel that you fall short and seek improvement.

Obtaining knowledge from a book, seminar, mastermind, or podcast is not enough to create a change in your life, but the consistent use and application of the information acquired from those sources, will make the difference.

As I mentioned previously, I was cuffed and bound in a world of uncertainty with no direction. For decades, I struggled to discover who I was and who God called me to be. That was definitely a difficult period in my life but one I treasure. Once I was able to free my mind of self-imposed limiting beliefs that constantly bombarded me with debilitating thoughts, I then began to see my life change for the better. I wrote this book and shared my personal story in hopes of helping you to free yourself of your limitations so that you can claim your potential and go after your dreams. There is no more time to waste! *Awaken your perspective* and visualize yourself doing exactly what you want to do. Allow your inner child to fantasize again the way you did when you were five years old. Dream BIG! Imagine yourself winning and having everything that *you* want. If you want things to change for the better, then your perspective of yourself must change and *be better*. You have watched others live their desired aspirations, and now it's time to live yours.

People With Great Passion Can Make the Impossible Happen."
Unknown

One of the main reasons people remain cuffed, bound, and not living the lifestyle that they long for is because of a lack of clarity. But those days are over for you. It is time to unleash your passion and do what is in your heart! Don't set aside your passion because of someone else's opinion. Where would Jennifer Lopez (JLo) be if she had honored her mother's wishes and gone to college instead of acting school? What if rapper Eminem wouldn't have pursued his musical career and instead listened to his mom who encouraged him to continue working so that he could help pay the bills. And despite growing up in a trailer park, raised by an alcoholic mother and stepfather, Demetria (Demi) Moore dropped out of high school and left her family at the age of sixteen. She did odd jobs for years as she pursued her dreams of becoming an award winning actress.

Those examples may not resonate with you because in your mind you're probably thinking that these are well-known celebrities. But there are some people that I know personally right here in the United States in my hometown of Philadelphia, PA who discovered their purpose by following their passion. My cousin, Kevin Ghee, who started the police Academy with me, decided after working only seven years to leave the police department and follow his passion. Kevin took a chance on himself and purchased a one-way ticket to Los Angeles, CA to pursue his passion in the executive protection industry. Upon arrival, he found a security guard position which was only paying $95 an hour. But after a few years, Kevin became the head of security for a large Hollywood cable network.

Another successful friend is Minister Roslyn (Roz) Talley, who took her passion for helping people outside of the four walls of her local church, and started a prayer line on Facebook named, *24/365 Continuous Live Prayer*. Starting with just a few friends joining her in the spring of 2020, today there are more than 4,000 members from around the world, even as far as India. She has also added her own radio station, Real Change Radio where she continues to spread the Gospel.

Then there is Jai Gordon, who left her job as a police offi-cer to fulfill her passion as a fitness and wellness coach. Her mission is to provide health and fitness education to the Black community and in schools where it is greatly needed. During her career, Jai saved her money to fund her dream, and in September, 2018, GymRatz went from being housed in her basement to new property in the heart of childhood neighborhood where she offers classes for children and adults[12].

Lastly, there's Mr. Ronald (Mitch) Mitchell, who was a highly respected husband, father and entrepreneur in his com-munity. He and his sister were raised by their mother in

---

[12] *(https://gymratzathleticsom)*

a small town in Maryland. After graduating high school, Ronald decided not to settle for becoming a farm-hand or a factory worker as many black men did in the Jim Crow south. Therefore, with the blessings of his mother, he moved north to Philadelphia, Pa to attend barber school. After graduating, he was hired by Mr. Alston, who became a father figure and groomed him to become a businessman.

In 1965, Mr. Mitchell branched out on his own and rented a building that became the iconic Mitchell's Barbershop. Now a young newlywed and father, the new business owner received a rude awakening when he only made $14 in his first week of service. Wondering how he would feed his family, Mr. Mitchell asked his former boss and mentor, Mr. Alston for his job back. Despite the slow start, he was encouraged to wait at least a month to see if things would improve. Not only did he survive a month, Mitchell's Barber Shop lasted 55 years and became the longest tenured black-owned business in the community. During that time, Mr. Mitchell managed his shop working alongside his wife, son, and two daughters who were all licensed barbers. He also mentored and groomed other barbers in which three of them went on to open their own shops in the community. "Mr. Mitch," as he was affectionately known, passed away in December of 2017, and left a legacy that touched many generations.

Remember that you too were created to do something

special, and God has given you the gift to do whatever He's called you to do. And whatever he called you to do is *your* purpose. Whenever you are operating in your purpose, whether it's teaching, singing, leading, playing the piano, professional sports, renovating houses, styling hair, or any other thing, you feel the passion in your heart. And what God puts in your heart, He also gives you the potential to succeed at. As the late, motivational speaker, Zig Ziglar once said, "You don't have to be great to get started, but you have to start to be great." This is also true for you. Start by setting your goals, change any self-destructive habits and develop new productive ones that will help you to become disciplined and consistent. Hire a coach to assist you in formulating a plan and hold you accountable to help you reach your destination. Create a vision board so you can constantly see your aspirations and affirm them to be yours. Also, align yourself with people who will inspire, empower, and ignite the hunger in you, and celebrate with you when you reach the finish line.

LIVING YOUR DREAMS

"Don't dream your life, but live your dream."

Mark Twain

An American writer, Humorist, and Entrepreneur

It has been my honor to write this book with the hopes that it will move you from where you are right now to where you want to go. If ever I can help you get there, don't hesitate to reach out or ask. I know all too well that when we take action and move outside our comfort zone, we need support and guidance. If I can be that for you let me know. I am often speaking at events, church groups, and even in prison and schools. I counsel people one on one and assist them in uncuffing their old beliefs to embrace new ones that will lead them to use their potential and live their dreams. I believe we all should be living as God intended us to be, and he put me here on this earth as a guide, support, and to be a beacon to help others achieve their dreams. Helping you to uncuff your potential is why I am here.

If you'd like to know more about me, you can read about my personal Ignite Moment™ in the international best-selling book, *Ignite The Hunger In You* with world-renowned motivational speaker Les Brown. Myself and 34 other authors shared how we were transformed and inspired to live our best lives despite our hardships and setbacks. When working with Les he told me that *the world is waiting on my story to help them find their voice and the power that lies within.* He was amazed and pleased to learn that as a police officer, I had such a zeal to help people uncuff their potential, and find their freedom. Listening to Les taught me that I too could go as far as I could imagine, and he showed me how to tell my story and speak with confidence.

That wisdom has uncuffed more in me and inspired me to continue to encourage, inspire, and empower people around the world to uncuff their dreams, talents, brilliance, uniqueness, and whatever other gift God has graced them with.

If you'd like to learn even more about yourself, I invite you to download my workbook, "5 Insightful Tips for Self-Discovery[13]. It will guide you through five practical ideas that will help you find your purpose and get you on your path to greatness. It will also cause you to look at your life from a perspective that focuses on the things you *love* to do, versus the things you feel bound to do. It will also show you how you can get started doing the things you love doing and the inspiration to help you stay on course.

You will find it on my website[14], resources from my books, speaking events, and a link to my monthly newsletter. Also, I will include a link to the first chapter of my next book entitled, *Uncuff My Sons, a Guide for Single Women Trying to Raise Boys.*

My goal is that once you close this book you will be ready to take a leap of faith and go after the life God has designed for you. Believing in yourself and taking that first step will lead to the next step, and then the next. And once you get

---

[13] Available at https://documentclouddobeom/link/review?uri=urn:aa-id:scds:US:d7102a33-30f6-42ad-9eb2-6bbec0833e90

[14] https://uncuffedpotentialom/

the momentum towards your destiny, only you can stop your progress.

You now hold the keys to uncuff your potential! Go out and unlock your dreams!!

RESOURCES

- https://pennsylvania.hometownlocator.com
- https://www.schooldigger.com/go/PA/schools
- https://www.schooldigger.com/go/PA/schools
- https://www.insightintodiversity.com/povertys-long-lasting-effects-on-students-education-and-success
- https://collectivehub.com/2017
- https://www.efe.com/efe/english/entertainment/lady-gaga
- www.cnbc.com
- www.google.com
- www.cnbc.com
- (https://wwwebmdom/mental-health/what-is-a-people-pleaser
- wwworldometersnfo
- https://gymratzathleticsom
- 5 Insightful Tips for Self-Discovery available at https://documentclouddobeom/link/review?uri=urn:aaid:scds:US:d7102a33-30f6-42ad-9eb2-6bbec0833e90
- https://uncuffedpotentialom

ABOUT THE AUTHOR

Curtis Ghee has served 29 years in the Philadelphia Police Department as a patrolman, a community relations officer, and a peer counselor to his fellow officers. In his years of service, Curtis witnessed a lot of trauma and dysfunction in the lives of many of the residents in the communities he served. Over time, he would also discover that not only the people that were being arrested had issues, but there was also trauma and challenges in the lives of some of his fellow comrades. Curtis realized that civilians and police officers alike were mentally and emotionally bound by their circumstances, and in some cases, in desperate need of being released from their own personal jail cells.

Seeing the correlation between physical incarceration and mental limitations that hindered both freedom and personal self-worth, Curtis was inspired to map out a program designed to help people find their freedom by using these (5) key principles: Perspective, Passion, Potential, Purpose, and Planning for personal success. He felt his own life experiences and dedication to others would be served by writing a book to help individuals uncuff their potential.

Curtis is an international best-selling author of the compilation book, Ignite the Hunger in You, featuring the legendary motivational speaker Les Brown. He is also a minister, loving husband, father, and grandfather. He and his wife, Falesha, are co-founders of Uncuffed Potential, Inc, a non-profit organization destined to help people find freedom from their limitations.

www.ingramcontent.com/pod-product-compliance
Lightning Source LLC
Chambersburg PA
CBHW060521130626
46553CB00002B/589